When People Are

BIG

and GOD

Is Small

Resources for Changing Lives

A series published in cooperation with
THE CHRISTIAN COUNSELING AND EDUCATIONAL FOUNDATION
Glenside, Pennsylvania

Susan Lutz, Series Editor

Available in the series:

Unless otherwise indicated, Scripture quotations are from the HOLY BIBLE, NEW IN-TERNATIONAL VERSION. Copyright © 1973, 1978, 1984 by International Bible Society. Used by permission of Zondervan Bible Publishers. Italics indicate emphasis added.

Printed in the United States of America

Library of Congress Cataloging-in-Publication Data

Welch, Edward T., 1953–
    When people are big and God is small : overcoming peer pressure, codependency, and the fear of man / Edward T. Welch.
        p.   cm. — (Resources for changing lives)
    Includes biographical references.
    ISBN-10: 0-87552-600-4 (pbk.)
    ISBN-13: 978-0-87552-600-3 (pbk.)
        1. Interpersonal relations—Religious aspects—Christianity.
    2. Intimidation. 3. Fear—Religious aspects—Christianity. 4. Self-es-
teem—
    Religious aspects—Christianity. 5. Self-confidence—Religious aspects—
    Christianity.   I. Title.   II. Series.
    BV4597.52.W45   1997
    248.4—dc21   97-18713

When People Are
BIG
and GOD
Is Small

*Overcoming Peer Pressure,
Codependency, and the Fear of Man*

EDWARD T. WELCH

P&R

P U B L I S H I N G

P.O.BOX 817 • PHILLIPSBURG • NEW JERSEY 08865-0817

To my daughters,

Lindsay and Lisa

Contents

Acknowledgments

This book has been a team effort. I am especially indebted to the staff and faculty of the Christian Counseling and Educational Foundation (CCEF) in Philadelphia. I could not have written this volume without their sacrifice, prayers and spiritual sharpening. John Bettler, Director, and Paul Tripp, Academic Dean, were especially helpful in providing the time off, but the entire CCEF community contributed. David Powlison and Susan Lutz gave generously of their time and skill by carefully reviewing earlier drafts of the book. Their comments were invaluable.

A number of friends reviewed all or parts of the book, notably Beth Noble and Julie Vickers. They, along with other friends, were essential to the development of my biblical thinking.

My wife, Sheri, has been *the* catalyst for change in my life. Without her love and patience I would never have seen many of these biblical truths. Also, while I worked on the manuscript, she was always willing to drop what she was doing to read or think through a section with me. She provided insights that clarified both the grammar and biblical thought. And she knew when to take me to the beach.

CHAPTER 1

LOVE TANKS WITH A LEAK

"FOR a long time, I didn't have any self-esteem," William began. "The only time I felt good was when I had $100 sneakers and a $60 sweatshirt. If I didn't have them, I didn't want to go to school."

Who would have thought that beneath William's tough, cool image was an ego that could be crushed simply by cheap shoes or a generic sweatshirt? Too bad some of his enemies didn't know. They could have avoided a number of bruises, courtesy of William's fists. Little did they realize that William was a modern day Samson: his strength was in his shoes. Steal his shoes and you conquered the man.

Of course, his shoes weren't exactly the problem. The problem was William's reputation. It was what other people *thought* about his shoes—and therefore, him. Call it what you like—reputation, peer pressure, people-pleasing, codependency—William's life was controlled by other people. In that, he was no different from most anyone else.

My personal awakening to this problem came when I was a high-school senior. I had always been shy and self-conscious, controlled by what my peers thought (or *might* have thought), but I never considered it seriously until the day of the awards assembly.

I was up for an award, and I was scared to death I would get it!

The auditorium was bulging with over two thousand high-school juniors and seniors. From the back, where I liked to sit, it seemed a good mile or two up to the platform. All I could think of was what my classmates would think of me while I walked to the front. Would I walk funny? Would I trip going up the stairs? Would one person—I prayed it wouldn't be a girl I liked—think I was a jerk? What about those who were also nominated or who thought they were deserving? What would they think of me if I won instead of them? What would I ever say for a brief acceptance speech?

God, please don't let me get this! I prayed.

After a number of lesser awards were announced, the vice principal went to the podium to introduce the winner. He began with a short, somewhat cryptic biographical sketch. It didn't sound *exactly* like me, but it was generic enough to fit. I was starting to sweat, but I sat motionless for fear that someone would think I was getting interested. Finally the announcement came: "And the winner of this year's senior award is ... Rick Wilson!"

Rick Wilson! I couldn't believe it! Of all people. No one even thought he was a candidate!

You can imagine my reaction. Relief? No way. I felt like a total failure. *Now* what would people think of me? They knew I was up for the award, and someone else was chosen. What a loser I was.

Immediately my mind began spinning out justifications. *If I had worked at all this year, I would have won. I certainly had the potential, I just didn't want to win. I'm a late bloomer; when I get to college, I will show them.* I was ashamed to go back to class.

Pitiful, isn't it?

Later that day the events replayed in my mind. *What a mess!* I reflected. *I live like a frightened kid. I am so controlled by what other people think or might possibly think.* But that was about it. I didn't know where to go from there. I didn't have sufficient biblical resources to find any solutions to what I discovered about myself. As far as I could tell, there was no way out. This was my life. Self-consciousness, being controlled by the opinions of others, or whatever it was called, could only be managed, not cured. Perhaps future success would help. Or (and I thought this was quite clever) I could embellish one of the justifications that had crossed my mind earlier in the day. I could do well but never be wholeheartedly devoted to any particular task. Then when I wasn't successful and my self-esteem was in the Dumpster, I would rationalize that I *could* have been the best if I had worked harder. At least *I* could think I was okay, for what that was worth.

I had no answers, but the events of the day certainly brought these issues to the front of my mind. It was, at least, an awakening.

In college I tried to combat this beast with a few quasi-successes in academics and athletics, and I used the I-could-have-done-better-if-I-really-tried strategy, but this *thing* was ever-present. I was a Christian, but that didn't help me put up a fight. I still felt it. Every rejection, every perceived failure, every person I wanted to be noticed by who didn't notice me reminded me that I was still the kid sitting in the back of the high-school auditorium.

Okay in Christ

There were a few changes during my seminary days. They came during my first year when I had the opportunity to lead a Bible study on the book of Romans. I had already considered Romans' theme of justification by faith, but this time it seemed especially relevant because I made a connection between my dependence on the opinions of other people and justification by faith. My reasoning, certainly not original with me, was that I didn't have to measure up to the standards of others' opinions because God's opinion of me was rooted in the finished work of Jesus. In other words, even though I was a sinner, God loved me and made me righteous in his sight, so *who cared what other people thought?!*

This seemed to be the freedom I needed. I felt as if I was converted again. I didn't have to be concerned about the opinions of others. I simply had to be aware of God's opinion of me. I was a beloved son. A saint. Okay in Christ. Great!

Over the next few years I was still over-concerned about the opinions of others, but I would quickly remind myself that I didn't have to measure up to what they might be thinking.

Who cares what they think? I tried to persuade myself. *So what if they don't think I'm great? I have already measured up because of what Jesus did.* I figured that if Jesus thought I was great, that should be enough.

I *thought* my treatment was working. There were only a few moments when I would have my doubts. Sometimes I would think, *Is it really Christ that I am standing on, or am I standing on my perceived successes and the favorable opinions of others?* After all, other people were usually very affirming. Maybe I felt good about myself because *they* felt good about me. Or maybe I felt good about myself because I had done respectably in athletics and had decent grades, *compared to other people.* Maybe I had taken pride in my ministry aspirations, *compared to other people* and their seemingly lower spiritual goals. Maybe I found an identity in being "nice," or at least nicer than most of the people I knew. But aren't all people-pleasers nice? In short, perhaps I was still being ruled by the opinions of others, but since I was feeling fine, I wasn't very motivated to investigate further. I certainly wasn't going to talk to anyone else about it—that would have been too embarrassing.

Then I got married.

A *Great Awakening*

Marriage has been a privilege and blessing to me. It has also been the context for a surprising discovery. I found that being okay in Christ was not quite enough for me. When I was first married, I knew that Jesus loved me, but I also wanted my new wife to be absolutely, forever smitten with me. I *needed* love from her. I could finally handle small amounts of rejection from other people, but I felt paralyzed if I didn't have the love I needed from her. I needed *unconditional* love. If she didn't think I was a great husband, I would be crushed (and, as you might guess, a little angry).

This led to a second awakening. I suddenly realized that I had mutated into a walking love tank, a person who was empty inside and looking for a person to fill me. My bride was, indeed, gifted in being able to love, but no one could have possibly filled me. I think I was a love tank with a leak.

I tried the old biblical answers that had worked before my marriage, but they were of no use. They didn't go far enough. In fact, they became almost irrelevant. They reminded me of times when, after I'd been politely dumped by a girl, my parents would try to cheer me up with "We love you no matter what." I always appreciated their attempt, but, as all parents and children know, it didn't help. Sure, it was nice that my parents loved me, and it would have been much worse if they did *not* love me, but I wanted *somebody else* to love me too.

Since those days I have spoken with hundreds of people who end up at this same place: they are fairly sure that God loves them, but they also want or *need* love from other people—or at least they need *something* from other people. As a result, they are in bondage, controlled by others and feeling empty. They are controlled by whoever or whatever they believe can give them what they think they need.

It *is* true: what or who you need will control you.

Facing the "Fear of Man"

Many of the people I've talked to also had an awakening when they saw the controlling power of other people. They awoke to an epidemic of the soul called, in biblical language, "the fear of man." Although they were avowed worshippers of the true God, below the surface they feared other people. That is not to say that they were terrified by or afraid of others (although sometimes they were). "Fear" in the biblical sense is a much broader word. It includes being afraid of someone, but it extends to holding someone in awe, being controlled or mastered by people, worshipping other people, putting your trust in people, or needing people.

One additional note: Just as "fear" in the biblical sense is broadly defined, so too is the word "man." As used in Scripture, it includes men, women, and children. When I use the biblical expression "fear of man" in this book, I am not limiting my focus to the male gender. I am assuming, as the Bible does, that every person in our lives has the potential to control us.

However you put it, the fear of man can be summarized this way: We replace God with people. Instead of a biblically guided fear of the Lord, we fear others.

Of course, the "fear of man" goes by other names. When we are in our teens, it is called "peer pressure." When we are older, it is called "people-pleasing." Recently, it has been called "codependency." With these labels in mind, we can spot the fear of man everywhere.

➤ Have you ever struggled with peer pressure? "Peer pressure" is simply a euphemism for the fear of man. If you experienced it when you were younger, believe me, it is still there.

It may be submerged and revealed in more adult ways, or it may be camouflaged by your impressive résumé (your perceived successes).

➤ Are you over-committed? Do you find that it is hard to say no even when wisdom indicates that you should? You are a "people-pleaser," another euphemism for the fear of man.

➤ Do you "need" something from your spouse? Do you "need" your spouse to listen to you? Respect you? Think carefully here. Certainly God is pleased when there is good communication and a mutual honor between spouses. But for many people, the desire for these things has roots in something that is far from God's design for his image-bearers. Unless you understand the biblical parameters of marital commitment, your spouse will become the one you fear. Your spouse will control you. Your spouse will quietly take the place of God in your life.

➤ Is self-esteem a critical concern for you? This, at least in the United States, is the most popular way that the fear of other people is expressed. If self-esteem is a recurring theme for you, chances are that your life revolves around what others think. You reverence or fear their opinions. You need them to buttress your sense of well-being and identity. You need them to fill you up.

➤ Do you ever feel as if you might be exposed as an impostor? Many business executives and apparently successful people do. The sense of being exposed is an expression of the fear of man. It means that the opinions of other people—

especially their possible opinion that you are a failure—are able to control you.

➤ Are you always second-guessing decisions because of what other people might think? Are you afraid of making mistakes that will make you look bad *in other people's eyes?*

➤ Do you feel empty or meaningless? Do you experience "love hunger"? Here again, if you need others to fill you, you are controlled by them.

➤ Do you get easily embarrassed? If so, people and their perceived opinions probably define you. Or, to use biblical language, you exalt the opinions of others to the point where you are ruled by them.

➤ Do you ever lie, especially the little white lies? What about cover-ups where you are not technically lying with your mouth? Lying and other forms of living in the dark are usually ways to make ourselves look better before other people. They also serve to cover our shame before them.

➤ Are you jealous of other people? You are controlled by them and their possessions.

➤ Do other people often make you angry or depressed? Are they making you crazy? If so, they are probably the controlling center of your life.

➤ Do you avoid people? If so, even though you might not say that you *need* people, you are still controlled by them. Isn't a hermit dominated by the fear of man?

➤ Aren't most diets, even when they are ostensibly under the heading of "health," dedicated to impressing others? The desire for the "praise of men" is one of the ways we exalt people above God.

➤ Have all these descriptions missed the mark? When you compare yourself with other people, do you feel good about yourself? Perhaps the most dangerous form of the fear of man is the "successful" fear of man. Such people think they have made it. They have more than other people. They feel good about themselves. But their lives are still defined by other people rather than God.

A *Universal Problem*

Don't think that this is simply a problem for the shy, mousy types. Isn't the angry person or the person who tries to intimidate also controlled by others? Any form of one-upmanship qualifies. What about the business executive who is working to be more productive than an associate in order to get ahead? The endless jockeying of egos in the corporate board room is an aggressive version of fear of man. And do you think that the super-confident, superstar athlete is somehow above seeking the good opinions of fans and sports writers? Aggressively asserting that you don't need anyone is just as much an evidence of the fear of man as the more timid examples we have seen. Fear of man comes in these packages and many others.

Does it include you yet? If not, consider just one word: evangelism. Have you ever been too timid to share your faith in Christ because others might think you are an irrational fool?

Gotcha.

Fear of man is such a part of our human fabric that we should check for a pulse if someone denies it.

In the United States we are on the tail end of a revolution that included scores of books on codependency. For years every book that had the word "codependency" in the title was a guaranteed best seller. Melodie Beattie, for example, made millions with *Codependent No More*. She obviously hit on a topic that was important to many people, yet it was basically the fear of man in a secular garment. Melody Beattie talked about the problem in terms of being controlled by or dependent on other people, and her prescription was to love yourself more.

The Search for a Biblical Response

That approach sounded a little shallow to the evangelical world, so many Christians responded by saying that a better treatment for codependency is to know that *God* loves you more than you think. God can fill you with love, so you don't have to be filled by other people.

This certainly is better than the exhortation to love yourself more, but—and this might sound controversial—even this answer is incomplete. The love of God can be a profound answer to just about any human struggle, but sometimes we can use it in such a way that it becomes a watered down version of profoundly rich truth. For example, sometimes, because of shortcomings in us rather than Scripture, this answer misses the call to "consider others better than yourselves" (Phil. 2:3), or it ignores personal repentance. Sometimes it still allows us and our needs to be at the center of the world, and God becomes our psychic errand boy given the task of inflating our self-esteem.

We need to go further in searching the Scripture so that we can truly understand the nearly universal experience of the fear of man. The purpose of this book is to take that next step. Along the way we will meet people such as Abraham and Peter, who slipped into the chasm of the fear of man and brought others down with them. We will look at the subtle ways in which that fear surfaces in our lives. We will see that the codependency writers were right—this *is* a national epidemic. Then we will find God's way out.

Here are some of the themes we will explore.

> ➤ To really understand the roots of the fear of man, we must begin to ask the right questions. For example, instead of "How can I feel better about myself and not be controlled by what people think?" a better question is "Why am I so concerned about self-esteem?" or "Why do I have to have someone—even Jesus—think that I am great?" These are topics we will look at from many angles throughout this book, but included in the answer is the fact that we need a way to think *less often* about ourselves. We'll talk about why—and how.

> ➤ The most radical treatment for the fear of man is the fear of the Lord. God must be bigger to you than people are. This antidote takes years to grasp; in fact, it will take all of our lives. But my hope is that the process can be accelerated and nurtured through what we will study in this book.

> ➤ Regarding other people, our problem is that we *need* them (for ourselves) more than we *love* them (for the glory of God). The task God sets for us is to need them *less* and love them *more*. Instead of looking for ways to manipulate others, we will ask God what our duty is toward them. This perspective does not come naturally to any of us, and many of us need to look at this truth from several angles before we can see it. But the conviction of this book is that this truth is another of Scripture's divine paradoxes—the path of service is the road to freedom.

PART ONE   *How and Why*
            We Fear Others

Part One of this book will explore the Bible's perspective on the fear of man in order to help you do three things:

- ➤ Step 1: Recognize that the fear of man is a major theme both in the Bible and in your own life.

- ➤ Step 2: Identify where your fear of man has been intensified by people in your past.

- ➤ Step 3: Identify where your fear of man has been intensified by the assumptions of the world.

CHAPTER

"People Will See Me"

Fear of man will prove to be a snare, but whoever trusts in the
LORD is kept safe. —*Proverbs 29:25*

IF needing or fearing people is as universal a problem as it seems, then we would expect Scripture to be filled with rich descriptions and in-depth teaching about it. And that is exactly what we find. One of the Bible's dominant questions is, Whom will you fear (need, be controlled by)? Will you fear God or people? Scripture gives three basic reasons why we fear other people, and we will look at each one of them in turn.

1. We fear people because they can expose and humiliate us.
2. We fear people because they can reject, ridicule, or despise us.
3. We fear people because they can attack, oppress, or threaten us.

These three reasons have one thing in common: they see people as "bigger" (that is, more powerful and significant) than God, and, out of the fear that creates in us, we give other people the power and right to tell us what to feel, think, and do.

STEP 1   *Recognize that the fear of man is a major theme both in the Bible and in your own life.*

The Fear That Comes from Shame

One reason we fear other people is that they can expose or humiliate us. That was apparent from the beginning. Immediately after the sin of Adam and Eve, "the eyes of both of them were opened, and they realized they were naked" (Gen. 3:7). This is the debut of the fear of other people. Shame-consciousness. Being exposed, vulnerable, and in desperate need of covering or protection. Under the gaze of the holy God and other people. God could see our disgrace, and other people became a threat because they too could see it. Their perceived opinions could now dominate our lives. The story of Scripture quickly became one in which people frantically looked to hide and protect themselves from the gazes of God and other people.

Shame from Sin

It was first apparent with *the look* from the other person. After that came the even more penetrating look from God. Both were so disturbing that Adam and Eve hid, and we are still hiding today. Certainly Adam and Eve knew they were naked before they sinned, and there is every reason to believe that, in their state of innocence, they looked admiringly on the physical appearance of the other. But this look was different. It could see a deeper nakedness, or at least the one being observed *felt* more exposed. The eyes of the other person became piercing lights, seeing body and soul, seeing the ugliness of sin. The feeling of being exposed, once completely foreign, was now the *only* thing they felt. They were *seen* by the other, and what was now seen was shameful. Once admirable in their innocence and beauty, their souls were now grotesque.

They tried coverings, but even animal skins were incapable of alleviating this deeper shame. What was once a blessing—knowing and being known—was now a curse. What was once a loving meeting of the eyes now became impolite and intrusive.

At the moment of Adam's sin, shame—that is, "What will *they* think of me?" and "What will *God* think of me?"—became a cornerstone of human experience.

From Genesis on, nakedness, or the shame of being exposed to others, became one of the great curses in Hebrew culture. It was a profound curse because it symbolized the deeper, spiritual nakedness and shame that needed covering. It symbolized that apart from God's covering, we stand naked before him. Noah cursed the progeny of Ham because Ham had gazed upon his father's nakedness, perhaps laughing at his father or ridiculing him. When Job was in the midst of his greatest misery, he spoke of his dread and cried, "Naked I came from my mother's womb, and naked I will depart." He was not simply resigned to the idea of death; instead, he acutely sensed that his shame was exposed and he was under the curse. The prophet Amos used the same imagery when he foretold the horrific judgment that would come on Israel by saying, "Even the bravest among warriors will flee naked on that day" (Amos 2:14–16).

Shame from Being Victimized or Sinned Against

Throughout human spiritual history, a second form of shame emerged. Original shame was simply the result of our sin. It was the result of being unclean and naked before the holy God, and it was usually experienced in our relationship with others. But overlaid on our sin-shame there soon appeared another form of shame that intensified original shame. It was the result of being sinned *against*, victimized or dishonored by others.

This second form of shame can be "caught" by contact with something unclean. For example, when Dinah was raped by Shecum, she was "defiled" (Gen. 34:5). This does not mean that

Dinah was responsible for what happened to her. The point is that even though she had not sinned, there is a sense in which her purity was marred.

If a man committed adultery with another man's wife, the innocent spouse would be shamed or dishonored, literally "made naked" by another's sin (e.g., Lev. 20:11, 17, 19, 20, 21). Unruly children brought shame and disgrace on their parents (Prov. 19:26). Even the temple was defiled because unclean men entered it (Ps. 79).

A similar thing happened when an Israelite touched the carcass of an animal that was declared unclean. Those who touched it, even accidentally, had to wash their clothes and were considered unclean until the evening (Lev. 11:24).

Therefore, there are two ways that we can become naked. The first is the self-imposed nakedness that is due to our sinful nature and our personal sin. The second is other-imposed nakedness that we experience because of the sin of other people. Unfortunately, this victimization-shame feels identical to the shame we feel from our own sin, even though the cause is very different. Victims feel embarrassment, humiliation, and disgrace because of the sins of others against them. They feel unclean, naked, and without access to covering. They feel as if they are under the all-knowing gaze of others, and they fear people. But, theologically, there is a big difference between the two.

➤ Sin-shame is something we bring on ourselves; victimization-shame is done to us.

➤ Everyone has the experience of sin-shame, but not everyone has this shame intensified by victimization-shame.

Shame from being sexually victimized is the best known example of victimization shame. Women who have been sexually violated can feel overwhelmed by what they perceive as the gaze of God and others.

"I feel like I have a neon sign across my forehead that says, 'I have been raped by my uncle,'" said one woman. She could be a spokesperson for thousands of others.

"I am afraid to open my mouth around other people," said another victim. "If I open my mouth, black slime will come out."

These heart-wrenching expressions are clearly the consequence of victimization-shame, but we must remember that such experiences do not exclude sin-shame, which is a universal condition. Victimization-shame usually *intensifies* pre-existing sin-shame. I have met very few who struggled with shame from victimization alone. Instead, such victims need biblical guidance in how to deal with their own sins, as well as their experience of being sinned against. Sometimes they have sins they must confess; sometimes they must learn to believe the promise of forgiveness of sins. Either way, it would be cruel to neglect their sin-shame because before God, we *all* must deal with it, and at some level our consciences know it. Therefore, in the following discussion on shame, I will combine the two categories of sin-shame and sinned-against shame. I will separate them later, but for now, consider the following examples of shame to be sin-shame that, in some cases, is intensified by victimization.

Shame in Today's World

Where do we find shame in today's secularized culture? Look at our bookshelves. Shame is so present in modern literature that it verges on the trendy and is perhaps in danger of—no pun intended—overexposure. *The Mask of Shame* by Leon Wurmser, *Shame and Pride* by Donald Nathanson, and *No Place to Hide* by

Michael Nichols are samples of the more technical discussions on shame.

You may not have heard of these books, but you are more likely to be familiar with shame's less technical form—self-esteem. Shame, and its feeling of disgrace before God and others, surfaces in our culture as low self-esteem, with its feelings of worthlessness. Shame and low self-esteem are both rooted in Adam's sin. They both are governed by the perceived opinions of others, and they both involve "not feeling good about ourselves." The only difference is that our word "shame" still retains the idea that we are ashamed before God as well as before other people, while self-esteem is seen as strictly a problem between ourselves and other people, or a problem just within ourselves. Low self-esteem is a pop version of biblical shame or nakedness. It is secularized shame.

When you realize that "shame" is almost interchangeable with "low self-esteem," it becomes difficult to find a book that does *not* discuss it. From Gloria Steinem's *Revolution from Within: A Book of Self-Esteem,* to every elementary school curriculum in the United States, America seems to have concluded that low self-esteem is the root of every problem. When I attended my first PTA meeting, I was informed that the chief objective of the elementary school my daughter was attending was to bolster self-esteem—and the parents gave a rousing ovation. Everyone believed that the core problem of childhood was being addressed.

I did not applaud. Instead, my wife and I had to decide whether we would keep our daughter in that school. Doesn't the teaching on self-esteem and its emphasis on *self* seem to make the problem worse? That was certainly my experience. When I tried to raise my own self-esteem, it just led to painful self-consciousness and further individualism. Even from a secular perspective, the self-esteem teaching seems suspect. Don't we do children a disservice by showering them with unearned approval? The self-respect the schools are seeking to bestow comes only as a person develops a growing ability to meet difficult tasks, risk failure, and overcome obstacles. You can't simply confer self-esteem upon another person. To assume that other people can control our view of ourselves is what creates low self-esteem in the first place!

But even with all the crazy ways that popular books try to inflate our self-esteem, there is a biblical message in it all. The massive interest in self-esteem and self-worth exists because it is trying to help us with a real problem. The problem is that we really are not okay. There *is* no reason why we should feel great about ourselves. We truly *are* deficient. The meager props of the self-esteem teaching will eventually collapse as people realize that their problem is much deeper. The problem is, in part, our nakedness before God.

There are other ways that shame can creep to the surface, too.

➤ Even with all the pornography and nudity that is part of Western culture, there remains the taboo on nudity. Why? Because it is a symbol of our need for deep, spiritual covering. The clothes we wear are an almost undeniable support of this biblical doctrine.

➤ We can be singing with all our heart when we are by ourselves, driving to work, radio blasting. But if someone happens to see us, we are embarrassed. It doesn't matter that the person who saw us was completely anonymous, never to be seen again. He or she still saw us and briefly reminded us of the deeper fear of being exposed.

➤ We have unwritten but clearly understood rules about how long to look at someone. Brief "eye contact" is courteous, but staring is impolite and can provoke embarrassment or even hostility. Women complain that men treat them as objects by staring at them; they feel as though they are being undressed.

➤ Even hallucinations tell the story of being "under the gaze." Throughout the world, a common hallucination is of eyes fixated on the hallucinator—eyes that follow you, penetrating eyes, dangerous eyes.

➤ Have you noticed how often the evangelical church emphasizes honesty and openness? It needs to be a continuing refrain because we don't like to be open. We prefer walls of self-protection even as Christians.

Hiding—and Spying

In the United States, a common metaphor that people use to describe themselves is a variation on covering the face in shame: we are people behind walls. "The walls are ten feet thick. Nobody can come in, and I can't get out." These desperate coverings isolate, but they also protect us from the gaze of other people. In practice, these walls can be built with thousands of different materials: money, fame, athletic accomplishment, jobs, and busyness. Nothing man-made, however, can truly cover shame.

A curious feature of most of these walls is the way they allow us to see other people. The thick walls apparently have small cracks or windows that allow us to see outside. We want to hide, but we also want to *spy*. Spying might reveal the vulnerability of others so that we can believe that they are no different from us (or even not as good as us). Disgrace wants company. On the other hand, it might reveal someone who is strong and can be our hero. With a hero, we might feel less isolated because we can enter into a safe fantasy relationship.

Fantasy is a popular past-time behind these walls. For example, Paula managed her world with fantasy, but you would never have known it. She was a successful, single, Christian woman. She had a great job with lots of responsibility and plenty of affirmation by the CEO. She was active in the church and was liked by everyone. But in the evenings, she lived with her fantasy hero husband and fantasy children. One reason she developed her fantasy world was because it gave her what she wanted. Another reason was that it gave her relationships without the risk of being known.

Bill's struggle followed a similar pattern. "I want to have my needs met, but I don't want to be exposed. I don't want anybody to really know me." So, to create a world that seemed safe, he indulged in pornography and masturbation.

Fantasy has been part of my own world, too, I confess. One recent example: I am relatively coordinated from the waist up, but my feet are useless. Too many years of swimming, I think. Coincidentally, my wife, Sharon, is coordinated all over, and she enjoys dancing. God, I think, did this to humble me.

Do you know what happened the last time we came home from a party where I tried to dance with my wife? My mind began to roam; I began to fantasize that I was a great dancer. My fantasy was that I walked casually out onto the dance floor, just a regular guy, and all of a sudden I was John Travolta. People were amazed, my wife thought I was great. . . . You get the idea.

It was funny or pitiful, depending on how you look at it. My point is that this relatively harmless fantasy is filled with fear of man, shame, and pride. It is fear of man because I am consumed with what other people might think of my klutziness. It is shame, especially the more secularized version, because I'm not feeling too good about myself. I'm feeling exposed before other people, believing that only a real jerk would be that hopeless on the dance floor. It is pride because I want to be perceived as great—at least in something.

That's the paradox of self-esteem: Low self-esteem usually means that I think too highly of myself. I'm too self-involved, I feel I deserve better than what I have. The reason I feel bad about myself is that I aspire to something more. I want just a few minutes of greatness. I am a peasant who wants to be king. When you are in the grips of low self-esteem, it's painful, and it certainly doesn't feel like pride. But I believe that this is the dark, quieter side of pride—thwarted pride.

Our hearts are certainly busy while we hide and spy.

Have you wondered why certain TV shows or magazines are so popular? Don't they offer us a brief opportunity to spy on others from behind our walls of shame? They let us see the disgrace of others, and that normalizes our own. Or they let us identify with our heroes, so we can briefly feel better about ourselves.

It is as if the modern person is a peeping Tom. While the peeping Tom is looking at someone through a keyhole, he is also being watched by another voyeur, who is being watched by another, who is being watched by another.

The Midnight Hour

In the early 1800s, Danish philosopher Soren Kierkegaard observed people whose lives consisted of hiding and spying. Rather than walls, they used masks.

> Do you not know that there comes a midnight hour when everyone has thrown off his mask? Do you believe that life will always let itself be mocked? Do you think you can slip away a little before

midnight to avoid this? Or are you not terrified by it? I have seen men in real life who so long deceived others that at last their true nature could not reveal itself; I have seen men who played hide and seek so long that at last in madness they disgustingly obtruded upon others their secret thoughts which hitherto they had proudly concealed.[1]

He is right. Everyday is Halloween. Putting on our masks is a regular part of our morning ritual, just like brushing our teeth and eating breakfast. The masquerade, however, is anything but festive. Underneath the masks are people who are terrified that there will be an unveiling. And, indeed, the masks and other coverings will one day be removed. There will be an eternal unveiling. But it is not so much the eyes of other people that we ought to fear. After all, other people are no different from ourselves. Kierkegaard points to a deeper fear: the eyes of God. If the gaze of man awakens fear in us, how much more so the gaze of God. If we feel exposed by people, we will feel devastated before God.

To even think of such things is too overwhelming. Our hearts tremble at the thought, and we do everything we can to avoid it. One way to avoid God's eyes is to live as if fear of other people is our deepest problem—*they* are big, not God. This, of course, is not the case. Fear of people is often a more conscious version of being afraid of God. That is, we are more conscious of our fear of others than our fear of God. Granted, fear of others *is* a real phenomenon. We really are afraid of the thoughts, opinions, and actions of other people. But under that we hide as best we can the more desperate fear of God. For example, notice the biblical version of Kierkegaard's masquerade.

---

1 From "Either/Or," in *A Kierkegaard Anthology,* ed. Robert Bretall (Princeton, N.J.: Princeton University Press, 1946), 99.

Jesus turned and said to them, "Daughters of Jerusalem, do not weep for me; weep for yourselves and for your children. For the time will come when you will say, 'Blessed are the barren women, the wombs that never bore and the breasts that never nursed!' Then 'they will say to the mountains, "Fall on us!" and to the hills, "Cover us!" ' " (Luke 23:28–30)

When Christ returns, those who are naked will prefer being covered by the boulders of Jerusalem's mountains to being exposed before the holy gaze of God.

God's Answer

Of course, God has an answer to this fear, and we will consider it in more detail shortly. The gospel is the story of God covering his naked enemies, bringing them to the wedding feast, and then marrying them rather than crushing them. King David, knowing about this coming good news, said, "O LORD, you have searched me and you know me" (Ps. 139:1). God's gaze—a curse to those who were naked—was to him a blessing. It is a protection for those who have had their guilt atoned for and their sins covered.

But being afraid of God might still be apparent, and with good reason. For those who have been covered with the righteousness of Jesus, this fear might not be the fear of being crushed. Instead, it might imitate the fear of David (Ps. 119:120) or Isaiah (Isa. 6) who, knowing they were sinners, trembled before the Most High God. It might be a fear associated with unconfessed sin. It might be fear associated with a lack of confidence in God's promises. Or it might be fear from feeling "unclean" as a result of being sinned against. As long as we are sinners, shame will be a familiar experience. We all know something about living behind walls and masks.

The answer seems simple: Remember that in Jesus' death, resurrection, and ascension, through faith he has covered you with righteous robes. He has removed your shame. This *might* be the only liberating teaching that the fearful person needs. However, my personal and counseling experience suggest that there are many times when a solution requires more than the reminder that Jesus died for us. For example, don't Paula, Bill, and I need something more? By that I am not saying that the gospel of Jesus is not enough. What I mean is that there are teachings implicit *in* the gospel that need attention. For example, from what do we need to repent? Do I love others in the name of Jesus, or am I more interested in protecting myself from them? How can I think less—as in less often—about myself?

There is much more to be said about the Bible's treatment of shame, but I'll summarize where we are now. The first biblical perspective on the fear of man is that it is the result of the nakedness that comes from sin. Because of sin still present within us, we experience embarrassment, shame, the feeling of being exposed and vulnerable. As a result, we try to protect ourselves and avoid the gaze of others. The ultimate problem *appears* to be the gaze of other people, but in reality the problem is within us and between God and ourselves. "Peer pressure" misses it. The ultimate problem is not the gaze of others. We classify it under the broader heading of "the fear of other people" only because this experience is most obvious when we are in their presence. For example, if the high school auditorium had been empty, or the vice principal had told me I had won an award over the phone, I would not have been embarrassed. The presence of others leaves us feeling exposed. However, even though it feels as if other people are doing the exposing, in reality we carry the shame with us all the time. Other people simply trigger its appearance.

The roots of shame-induced fear of man lie in our relationship with God. We stand ultimately under his penetrating, holy gaze. When we are particularly aware that we have violated God's righteousness, that gaze will condemn us unless we confess our sins and affirm that by faith "we have been made holy through the sacrifice of the body of Jesus Christ once and for all" (Heb. 10:10).

We also can be unholy because we have been defiled by the sins of others. In such cases, we are not directly culpable for our uncleanness, but we are still naked and need a covering for sin that only God can provide.

For Further Thought

1. If you still have a hard time seeing the fear of other people, consider ways that your private life is different from your public life. Are there sins that you can easily confess to God, but would be very difficult to share with another person? Are there things about yourself that you simply don't want people to know? These questions might reveal some of the roots of shame-driven fear of man in your life.

2. Consider some of the strategies you use to cover yourself, and remember that most people wear multiple layers.

3. Have you ever heard the sermon illustration about the five men who received a prank call saying, "They know what you've done. Leave town immediately!"? By evening, four of them had left town. The reason they were controlled by the prank caller was that their consciences condemned them. Does your conscience condemn you? If so, confess your sin before God and ask him for power to change. A clear conscience is a great blessing and one way to begin to root out the fear of other people.

"PEOPLE WILL
REJECT ME"

CLOSELY related to the fear that people will expose us (shame-fear) is perhaps the most common reason we are controlled by other people: they can reject, ridicule, or despise us (rejection-fear). They don't invite us to the party. They ignore us. They don't like us. They aren't pleased with us. They withhold the acceptance, love, or significance we want from them. As a result, we feel worthless.

It might give you *some* encouragement to know that, although rejection-fear seems very modern, it has been a problem for a number of illustrious people throughout history. For example, Moses warned the leaders and judges of Israel about this very thing (Deut. 1:17). Moses knew that people reverenced the opinions of others, showed favoritism, or honored one person above another, fearing rejection from those who were considered more important. Such a human tendency would have been an especially important issue for Israel's judges. For example, if an Israelite had to judge a case involving a prominent metal worker, there might have been a certain amount of pressure to make the judgment light or waive the penalty altogether. Otherwise, the metal worker might have rejected the judge next time he asked to have his plow repaired. Do you see the problem? Judges could be controlled by a defendant if the defendant had something the judges wanted. In such situations people would become big and God's justice would become small.

I wonder how many of us fear (respect or reverence) those who have more money, more power, more education, more attractiveness. As a counselor I have witnessed, in my own ministry and in others', a kinder and more tentative approach when counseling potential financial donors than when counseling indigents for free.

King Saul is a specific biblical example of someone who experienced rejection-fear. In 1 Samuel 15, Saul was commanded to destroy completely the Amalekites. God then gave the armies of Israel grace to defeat these people, "but Saul and the army spared Agag [king of the Amalekites] and the best of the sheep and cattle, the fat calves and the lambs—everything that was good" (1 Sam. 15:9). When the prophet Samuel confronted Saul with his gross disobedience, Saul confessed his sin, but justified it. "I was afraid of the people and so I gave in to them" (1 Sam. 15:24).

There are two possible perspectives on Saul's justification. He really may have felt pressure by his generals to bring home some of the spoils of war, in which case his defense is inexcusable in light of God's endless warnings not to fear people. Or Saul reasoned that the fear of others was so common that Samuel would accept his excuse because it was such a human thing to do. After all, since it is part of our fabric, how can we be held responsible for it? Regardless of which alternative represents Saul's true motives, the fear of others had catastrophic results: it was the reason that Saul lost his kingdom.

The New Testament Pharisees shared King Saul's fear of rejection. They craved acceptance and approval from the people, and they were afraid they wouldn't get it. Many Pharisees boasted that they didn't believe in Jesus, and they even accused those who *did* of living under a delusion (John 8:45–50). Yet there were some leaders who could not ignore Jesus' authoritative teaching and miracles, and they quietly believed in him. In other words, they believed that Jesus was sent from God; he was the Messiah for whom they had hoped and prayed. With such a conviction, you would think that these leaders would become disciples immediately and seek to persuade the people to believe. Yet it didn't happen. Their faith quickly withered. Why? They feared confessing their faith because of the possible reactions of those in the synagogue, "for they loved praise from men more than praise from God" (John 12:42–43). They felt they needed the praise of people. They feared rejection more than they feared the Lord.

It all sounds too familiar. Sometimes we would prefer to die for Jesus than to live for him. If someone had the power to kill us for our profession of faith, I imagine that most Christians would say, "Yes, I am a believer in Jesus Christ," even if it meant death. The threat of torture might make people think twice, but I think most Christians would acknowledge Christ. However, if making a decision for Jesus means that we might spend years being unpopular, ignored, poor, or criticized, then there are masses of Christians who temporarily put their faith on the shelf. "Death is not imminent, so why hurry into such a rash decision?" "There will be time later to get things straight with God."

In other words, kill me, but don't keep me from being liked, appreciated, or respected.

Does that sound too harsh? Remember that one word: *evangelism.* I am sure that many teens would rather die than have their friends catch them hanging out with the church youth group or doing Christian drama on the streets. Aren't the most popular mission trips the ones that take us far from our own neighborhood?

Russia is easy; our own neighborhood is a constant challenge. Has *anyone* consistently had the boldness and clarity of Jesus in testifying about the gospel? Never. Has anyone consistently avoided the fear of man in evangelism? Certainly not. There is a "foolishness" inherent in the message of the cross. The clear proclamation of the gospel does not make us look good. It doesn't make us popular.

"Peer Pressure" and the Praise of God

The sin resident in the human heart (the fear of man) wields awesome power. The praise of others—that wisp of a breeze that lasts for a moment—can seem more glorious to us than the praise of God. Jesus himself told the Jewish leaders, "How can you believe if you accept praise from one another, yet make no effort to obtain the praise that comes from the only God?" (John 5:44).

Today we would be nice and call the Pharisees people-pleasers. We would say they "struggled with peer pressure." Since all of us are affected by it at one time or another, we are almost sympathetic toward such behavior. But this is perhaps the most tragic form of the fear of man. Teenagers are constantly making unwise decisions because of it. Adults, too, look to people for their cues. We wait for others to take initiatives of love. We spend too much time wondering what others may have thought about our outfit or the comment we made in the small group meeting. We see opportunities to testify about Christ, but we avoid them. *We are more concerned about looking stupid (a fear of people) than we are about acting sinfully (fear of the Lord).*

Jesus stood in stark contrast to this Pharisaic concern. He did not show favoritism; instead, he reached out to male and female, rich and poor, and all races and ages. His teaching was not done by first taking a poll of what was popular; instead, he spoke truth that was often unpopular but could penetrate the heart. "I do not accept praise from men," he said. Even his opponents could see this.

> "Teacher," they said, "we know that you are a man of integrity and that you teach the way of God in accordance with the truth. You aren't swayed by men, because you pay no attention to who they are." (Matt. 22:16)

Of course, these remarks were a form of flattery used to trap Jesus, but they were true nonetheless. It was part of Jesus' teaching with authority, and it was one of the features that distinguished his ministry from that of all the other Jewish leaders.

It also characterized the ministry of the apostle Paul. He exhorted his churches to be imitators of him as he was an imitator of Christ (1 Cor. 4:16; 1 Thess. 1:6). By this, he was encouraging his disciples to imitate his life and doctrine, an imitation that certainly included seeking the praise of God, not men (1 Thess. 2:4). Paul was not a people-pleaser. He was a people-lover, and because of that he did not change his message according to what others might think. Only people-lovers are able to confront. Only people-lovers are not controlled by other people. Paul even indicated to the Galatians that if he were still trying to please men, he would not be a servant of God (Gal. 1:10). That is how seriously he took the fear of man.

Not that this came naturally. Paul had the same fleshly instincts we do, and he knew it. As a result, he beseeched the churches to pray for him.

> Pray also for me, that whenever I open my mouth, words may be given me so that I will fearlessly make known the mystery of the gospel. . . . Pray that I may declare it fearlessly, as I should. (Eph. 6:19–20)

Chapter Three

Peter's Battle with the Fear of Man

Now to a more tragic example of the fear of other people.

Peter has become known for his impetuous style. Of all the disciples, he seemed the boldest. He would probably be the last person we would expect to struggle with the fear of man. But this malady is in the hearts of the bold *and* the timid.

How could he have denied the Lord? He had seen the miracles. He was given the Spirit who revealed to him that Jesus was the Christ. He was the rock. He witnessed the transfiguration! He loved Jesus. Denial was unthinkable. But he too was like us—a fellow sinner, spiritually inept apart from the constant work of the Holy Spirit. He too could exalt people so that they seemed bigger than Jesus himself.

On a cold night Peter was outside the house of the high priest while Jesus was being questioned inside. He was standing close to a fire with a group of officials and servants. "I don't know what you're talking about," he said when told he'd been seen with Jesus.

For Peter to make such a denial, we would assume that his confronter must have been a centurion, a Pharisee, or someone who could have executed him on the spot. His life must have been in great danger. But no, it was a girl. Not a woman of great influence, but a servant girl. Yes, she was a servant of the high priest, but the high priest was busy with his inquisition of Jesus. He certainly had no time for Peter. Another disciple, probably John, was even in the house during Jesus' questioning. If they'd wanted to string up a disciple, the one inside would have been the obvious choice.

It would be gracious to think that Peter's life was in danger, but it wouldn't be true. He needed very little provocation to deny Christ.

A second time he was questioned, perhaps by the same servant girl, and he gave a similar response. But it was not a timid, don't-look-them-in-the-eye response. It was an adamant denial, punctuated with an oath. Surely Peter knew the seriousness of an oath. He knew Jesus' teaching from the Sermon on the Mount, "Let your 'yes' be 'yes,' your 'no' 'no.' " But sin made truth irrelevant at that moment. Fear of man is always part of a triad that includes unbelief and disobedience.

The third denial was even worse. "He began to call down curses on himself and he swore to them, 'I don't know the man.' "In other words, "May God Almighty curse me and my family if I am not speaking the truth." Fear of man is, indeed, a treacherous snare.

His timing couldn't have been worse. For at that moment, Jesus was able to see Peter, most likely as he was being taken from the high priest's house to the Sanhedrin. Jesus "looked straight at Peter."

For Peter, it was as if he was the first Adam. He felt the gaze of the holy and couldn't have felt more naked. There was no place to hide. As for Jesus, we can only guess what he was thinking.

What we know is that when Jesus appeared to his disciples, he delighted in demonstrating his awesome forgiveness to Peter. "Tell his disciples *and Peter,*" the angel announced after the resurrection. Then, perhaps on another cool night around a fire, Jesus countered Peter's three denials with three invitations to feed the flock, and he finished by saying, "Follow me" (John 21:15–19).

Having experienced the curse of the fear of man, having felt the gaze of the holy God, and having known such a rich, forgiving love, Peter undoubtedly had learned his lesson. Or so, I am sure, he thought. In spite of his strong faith and gifting by the Spirit, this remarkable man was humbled one more time because of his fear of other people. This time, the occasion for his people-pleasing was a meal with a group of Christians.

Peter was very aware that Gentiles were included in the gospel.

After his vision in Acts 10, he spent time with Gentiles like Cornelius. Later he apparently had a habit of meeting and eating with Gentiles. However, when Christian Jews who considered circumcision to be part of the gospel came to Peter, he separated himself from his gentile brothers and sisters. He treated them according to the Jewish custom rather than the Lord's command.

Why did he do this? He feared the circumcision group. What were the consequences? Other Jews, including Barnabas, were being led into the same error. Such "hypocrisy" was so serious that Paul opposed Peter face to face (Gal. 2:13).

Did Peter finally learn? This is perhaps the last personal anecdote we hear about Peter, because Luke, who wrote the book of Acts, followed Paul's later ministry more than Peter's. However, Peter's two epistles were most likely written after this event, and 1 Peter in particular suggests a connection between these events in Peter's life and the way he taught the early church.

> *Who is going to harm you if you are eager to do good? But even if you should suffer for what is right, you are blessed. "Do not fear what they fear; do not be frightened." But in your hearts set apart Christ as Lord. (1 Peter 3:13–14)*

"Don't fear people; fear the Lord," said Peter. He knew that the fear of man could be a snare.

People—Our Idol of Choice

What is it that shame-fear and rejection-fear have in common? To use a biblical image, they both indicate that people are our favorite idol. We exalt them and their perceived power above God. We worship them as ones who have God-like exposing gazes (shame-fear) or

God-like ability to "fill" us with esteem, love, admiration, acceptance, respect, and other psychological desires (rejection-fear).

When we think of idols, we usually think first of Baal and other
material, man-made creations. Next we might think of money. We
rarely picture our spouse, our children, or a friend from school. But
people are our idol of choice. They pre-date Baal, money, and power.
Like all idols, people are created things, not the Creator (Rom. 1:25),
and they do not deserve our worship. They are worshipped because
we perceive that they have power to give us something. We think they
can bless us.

When you think of it, idolatry is the age-old strategy of the
human heart. The objects of worship may change over time, but the
heart stays the same. What we do now is no different from what the
Israelites did with the golden calf. When the Israelites left Egypt,
they felt very vulnerable and needy (and were hard-hearted and
rebellious). Even though they had witnessed the power of God, they
felt afraid. They felt out of control. Their remedy was to choose an
idol over the true God. By doing this they were both opposing God
and avoiding him.

They opposed God by trusting in themselves and their own gods
rather than the true God. After all, they couldn't be absolutely
certain that God was going to bless the women with fertility. And
what about these other gods that seemed to have power to give
abundant crops? Just in case God was not enough, they started to
follow other gods. They thought idols would give them what they
wanted or felt they needed. They wanted a god they could control
and manipulate. They wanted nothing above themselves, including
God. God, they thought, would not be able to keep pace with their
desires, and so they looked for blessing and satisfaction in something they felt they could control. They wanted to do it their way
rather than God's. That is the height of rebellion.

In following other gods, the Israelites also wanted to *avoid* God. This suited them more than trusting him. The people of Israel had never before seen a display of holiness like they saw at Sinai. Such holiness left them feeling vulnerable and exposed. They became aware of their own shame. To deal with this holy terror, their rebellious hearts searched for a god that was tame. And the golden calf certainly was that.

So it is today. In our unbelief, we both oppose God and avoid him.

What is the result of this people-idolatry? As in all idolatry, the idol we choose to worship soon owns us. The object we fear overcomes us. Although insignificant in itself, the idol becomes huge and rules us. It tells us how to think, what to feel, and how to act. It tells us what to wear, it tells us to laugh at the dirty joke, and it tells us to be frightened to death that we might have to get up in front of a group and say something. The whole strategy backfires. We never expect that using people to meet our desires leaves us enslaved to them.

Sarah was a three-sport star at one of the best colleges in the country. Not only that, she was the sophomore captain of all three teams, and she had just been named co-winner of the college's best female athlete award. With such ability and recognition you would think that she was feeling pretty good about herself, but she was already worried about next year. The expectations of others were going to be even greater. How could she top what she had already accomplished? "She said she wanted to be the best girlfriend, the best athlete, the best student," related a good friend.

She wanted to quit one of her sports to alleviate some of the overwhelming stress in her life, but she was afraid to disappoint her teammates. Saying "no" to any friend was out of the question. "She wanted to please everybody and couldn't stop," one person observed. She could only think of one way out. Sarah took a .22-caliber rifle and shot herself in the chest.

People had become Sarah's idol. She needed their approval. She needed their friendship, and she felt utterly suffocated by possible disparaging opinions. The tragic reality was that Sarah was a slave to her idol, and tragedy accompanies such slavery. Sarah saw no other way to freedom.

For Further Thought

The purpose of these first two chapters is to reveal the fear of man in all of us. The reality behind this fear is much more profound than our present idea of being afraid. In the biblical sense, what we fear shows our allegiances. It shows where we put our trust. It shows who is big in our lives.

1. In your own words, what is the fear of man?

2. If the fear of others is as prevalent in our lives as the Bible suggests, make a list of the ways it is expressed in your life. You might want to start with some classic illustrations from when you were younger, but make sure you update it so that it includes last week.

3. Here are some other questions that might uncover the fear of man.

➤ What thoughts or actions do you prefer to keep in the dark? (This doesn't refer to getting dressed.) Lusts, animosities, certain habits ... Such activities most likely point to the fear of others.

➤ Have you noticed times when you cover up with lies, justifications, blaming, avoiding, or changing the subject? If so, you want to look better before people.

➤ Do you show favoritism? Do you respect the rich more than

the poor? The intelligent over the less intelligent? This is perhaps the most overlooked expression of the fear of other people. It shows that you respect one person above another.

4. What are some word pictures that describe you?

5. *Codependent No More* offered atrocious solutions for the fear of man, but it did a fine job describing it. Here are some of its descriptions. Try to reinterpret these descriptions and see the people-idols that lie behind them. Codependents may:

➤ think and feel responsible for other people.

➤ feel compelled to help people solve their problems.

➤ get tired of feeling like they always give to others but no one gives to them.

➤ blame, blame, blame.

➤ feel unappreciated.

➤ fear rejection.

➤ feel ashamed of who they are.

➤ worry whether other people like them or not.

➤ focus all their energy on other people and problems.

➤ threaten, bribe, beg.

➤ try to say what they think will please, provoke, or get them what they need.

➤ manipulate.

➤ let other people keep hurting them and never say anything.

➤ feel angry.

➤ feel like martyrs.

➤ be extremely responsible or irresponsible.

CHAPTER 4

"PEOPLE WILL PHYSICALLY HURT ME"

JANET was a victim of physical and sexual violence. From age seven to twelve, she was raped by her father. He stopped only because he got old and slow and Janet was able to elude him. But the violence didn't stop. During her early teen years her older brother would punch her until she was doubled over in pain. Yet black eyes and broken ribs could not get her to the hospital because her brother threatened to kill her if she told anyone.

She is thirty-five now. She has been married to a very supportive husband for eight years and has two children, a boy who is six and a girl who is three. Recently, she confronted both her father and her brother, and both men have acknowledged their offenses. Yet her husband's support and her perpetrators' confession have not shielded Janet from a host of different problems.

For example, when Janet speaks about either abuser, her attitudes fluctuate wildly. There are times when she craves a deeper relationship with them, but her passion is not for an adult friendship so much as it is to be a dependent child with them. She wants the love and affection from her father and brother that she never had when she was young. At other times she is very angry with them for what they have done and she wishes they were dead. At still other times she is terrified when she thinks about what happened and tries to distance herself from everyone because she feels as if every person she meets is a threat to her life.

Certainly, all these reactions are understandable in a woman who has been tragically victimized, but they also reveal that Janet's abusers continue to have a controlling influence in her life. Janet lives as though God is very small in comparison to these evil men.

We've already seen that the fear of other people comes out of *us*. It doesn't matter where we live or whom we lived with—the fear of man is a regular feature of our own sin-tainted hearts. But certain influences *can* leave us more prone to these sinful tendencies. They certainly did with Janet.

Janet's vulnerability to the fear of other people can be compared to the vulnerability to lust common in a person who is introduced to pornography at an early age. Lust is found in us all, but such a person *may* have to be particularly on guard against sexual lust. For some people sexual lust may be a fluctuating temptation; sometimes the battle is fierce, sometimes other battles seem more urgent. But for someone introduced to pornography, the battle may be constant. Such a person may have to enlist consistent prayer support and be prepared to fight the battle daily. In a similar way, those who have been threatened, attacked, or shamed by others tend to be more vulnerable to the fear of man, and they have to be especially vigilant.

STEP 2 *Identify where your fear of man has been intensified by people in your past.*

The Power of Words

Sexual and physical violence are clear examples of the way

destructive people in our pasts can make us more prone to fearing other people. But Scripture doesn't only speak of destructive deeds. It says that words, too, are powerful. How, I wonder, does cruel speech affect children? I know that children are immensely resilient, and I am not suggesting that one word will scar a child for life, but the Bible indicates that reckless words pierce like a sword (Prov. 12:18). The Bible never minimizes the effect of sinful words. It exposes them as firebrands that leave wounds that can go to the deepest parts of our being. They stand in stark contrast to the words of compassion and healing that the Lord offers to such victims.

I have seen children who have been crushed by the words of another. I have watched as some of them gradually became more reticent and withdrawn. They looked as if they were scared, always defensive and hypervigilant, as if they were in a battle. Is the sin of other people leaving them prone to a heightened version of the fear of man? In some cases, yes.

It usually takes more than one incident to ignite the flames of the fear of man. It is possible that one horribly timed criticism could do it, or perhaps some gossip about you that you overheard; but if your history made you more vulnerable to the fear of others, you were probably affected by a steady stream of discouraging words. In other words, day in and day out you heard something critical, demeaning, or unkind.

Maybe the unkind words weren't that frequent. I know a father who loses his temper perhaps once a month. When he does, everybody knows it, and anybody nearby is verbally attacked. After a half hour of being out of control, he comes back and apologizes to those he wounded. He acts like a binge drinker, but without the alcohol.

What do you think of this man? It would be nice to see his outbursts down to zero, but he *does* apologize. Things could be much worse. Yet I have witnessed changes in his one son. He is more

For example, when David was seized by the Philistines in Gath, he spoke about the hot pursuit of his attackers and his fear. Whenever he slept, he was uncertain as to whether or not he would wake. His response, however, was decidedly different from Abraham's. David was afraid, but he did not fear people over God. He said, "When I am afraid, I will trust in you. In God, whose word I praise, in God I trust; I will not be afraid. What can mortal man do to me?" (Ps. 56:3–4). God was David's rock and fortress. Yet Abraham, fresh from learning of God's promise to him, viewed the Egyptians as bigger than his God, and he lied as a way to deal with his fear. Although he is not an example of how to deal with the fear of others, Abraham at least shows us that it is common even among people of faith.

But why doesn't Abraham learn from this experience? A few chapters later, in Genesis 20, he uses the exact same ploy. Only one of the victims was different. Not only did he again put his wife in a situation where she could have been defiled, he also sinned against Abimelech, king of Gerar. Abimelech was not the powerful man that Pharaoh was, but he was a man of reputation and ruler of the region. That apparently was enough for Abraham, and so he asked his wife to resume the deception. Only God's forceful intervention kept Abimelech from adultery and Abraham from utter shame.

With this checkered past, this mingling of faith and fear, Abraham did not seem to be a good candidate for perhaps the most difficult test a person could undergo. Could he prioritize his fear of God to the point where he would obey even if it meant sacrificing his only son? It is one thing to have *your* life threatened, but it is something much more serious to have your *child's* life threatened. And this was the test that Abraham faced. But he never wavered. When told to sacrifice his son, Abraham was up early in the morning to obey the Lord! What father would have done that? Most of us would at least take a few hours to go for a quiet walk together or have a final game of catch. But Abraham recovered from his fear of man in a spectacular way when he was tested by God. When Abraham demonstrated his willingness to trust God even if it meant the death of his son, the angel of the Lord said, "Now I know that you fear God" (Gen. 22:12).

Fear Wins and a Generation Loses

Abraham's example of bold faith did not eradicate the fear of man from his descendants. Israel's history literally took a dramatic turn because of the Hebrews' fear that the Canaanites would physically hurt them. The people went from being on the verge of entering the Promised Land to wandering in the desert wilderness. In Numbers 13, a group of Israeli scouts had been commissioned to explore the land. In their report they indicated that, indeed, it was the Promised Land, "and it does flow with milk and honey" (Num. 13:27). But they were more in awe of the inhabitants of the land than they were in awe of their God, even though they had just witnessed that their God was the greatest of all gods in his confrontation with Pharaoh.

> But the people who live there are powerful, and the cities are fortified and very large.... We can't attack those people; they are stronger than we are.... We seemed like grasshoppers in our own eyes, and we looked the same to them. (Num. 13:28, 31, 33)

Moses' plea not to be afraid was ignored (Num. 14:9). And judgment for such unbelief was certain. God said,

> How long will they refuse to believe in me, in spite of all the miraculous signs I have performed among them? I will strike them down with a plague and destroy them, but I will make

you [Moses] into a nation greater and stronger than they.
(Num. 14:11–12)

Our jealous God demands that he alone be worshipped and exalted. To fear Pharaoh rather than the true God was idolatry. But because of Moses' gracious intervention on behalf of the people, God mercifully reduced their punishment. Instead of the utter annihilation of Israel, God prohibited one generation from entering the Promised Land. They would die as desert nomads, but their children would see the fulfillment of God's promise. This, indeed, was amazing grace.

When God's judgment was over and that generation was gone, Moses made one final appeal to the people. It was at a critical time, right before his own death. He was transferring power to Joshua, so the occasion was especially solemn. People were undoubtedly riveted to Moses' words. His warm, pastoral exhortation is the book of Deuteronomy. In it he called the people to absolute allegiance to God, and he warned them against covenant disobedience. He especially reminded the people to avoid the past error of fearing people more than God. Hadn't he always said, "Do not be afraid; do not be discouraged" (Deut. 1:21), and "Do not be terrified; do not be afraid of them" (1:29)? But during the wilderness wanderings the people had not listened, and the result had been a catastrophic defeat. *What they feared really did overtake them.*

So Moses continued with the warnings,

Do not be afraid of him [Og, king of Bashan]. (3:2)

Do not be afraid of them [all the kingdoms in the land]. (3:22)

Remember the day you stood before the LORD your God at

Horeb, when he said to me [Moses], "Assemble the people before me . . . that they may learn to revere [fear] me. . . ." (4:10)

Oh, that their hearts would be inclined to fear me [the LORD]. (5:29; also 6:2, 13)

You may say to yourselves, "These nations are stronger than we are; how can we drive them out?" But do not be afraid of them. (7:17–18)

Dozens of the same warnings and exhortations followed, all repeating the same theme: you are prone to fearing people who seem to be a threat to you; instead, fear God and God alone. At the end of the book of the covenant, Moses was not tired of repeating the warning. In Deuteronomy 31:6, Moses commanded the people, "Be strong and courageous. Do not be afraid or terrified because of them, for the LORD your God goes with you; he will never leave you or forsake you." He repeated this statement again, "Do not be afraid; do not be discouraged" (31:8). With that final encouragement, the sermon was over.

Two Faith-Filled Leaders

The book of Joshua begins the same way. Read Joshua 1:1–9 and note the exhortations. Three times during God's initial counsel to Joshua he says, "Be strong and courageous." "Have I not commanded you?" he asks. "Be strong and courageous. Do not be terrified: do not be discouraged, for the LORD your God will be with you wherever you go" (v. 9).

Ever the good student, Joshua later repeated these God-given commands when he confronted five captive kings. He told Israel, "Do not be afraid; do not be discouraged. Be strong and courageous" (10:25). His confidence was coupled with obedience—as it always must be—and he personally slew the five kings with his sword. Through such leadership, Joshua left the grandest of legacies: "Israel served the LORD throughout the lifetime of Joshua" (24:31).

David is another shining example of a man who feared God, not man. The psalms of David often revolve around one question: Whom will I fear, God or people? His answer, because he had come to know the living God, was rarely in question. "The LORD reigns forever" (Ps. 146:10). Mortal men die and their plans die with them (Ps. 146: 4). God was his shield (Ps. 3:3; 5:12; 7:10), his refuge (Ps. 5:11; 9:9), his strength (Ps. 118:14), and his rock, fortress, and deliverer (Ps. 18:2). When he was afraid, he remembered that people could have great power when compared to himself, but they had no power compared to his God.

For two years I worked in a veteran's hospital. During that time, I heard the stories of many war veterans and saw the consequences of war. Men would wake up from nightmares triggered by events that occurred forty years earlier. Some used drugs to quiet their fears and dull the mental pictures. Others isolated themselves as a way to protect themselves. Some of them seemed to be constantly vigilant, as if they never left the battle. Some used hair-trigger anger as their way to keep others at bay. If you had heard their combat stories, you probably would have thought that their threat-fear was natural.

I would say it was *almost* natural. King David was often threatened by enemies, and when he was threatened he too was afraid. But this was not exactly the fear of man, and it didn't provoke the fear of man. The fear of man is the sinful *exaggeration* of a normal experience.

Let me explain. We *should* be afraid when physically threatened. It is certainly not sinful for your adrenaline to be flowing when you are being fired upon. But fear of man is fear run amok. It might start with the very natural fear associated with being vulnerable and threatened. At times, however, this alarm is not regulated by faith. It becomes fear that is consumed with itself and for a time forgets God. It becomes a fear that, when activated, rules your life. In such a state, we trust for salvation in others.

Being afraid is not wrong in itself. As creatures living in a sinful world we *should* be afraid at times. The problem is when fear forgets God. This was Janet's experience and it was the experience of many of the veterans I have known.

David's psalms, therefore, are *not* illustrations of the fear of man. His fear was within godly parameters. In his fear he consistently turned to his King. He is an illustration that bad experiences don't *have* to provoke the sinful fear of people. But notice what David did. He was *constantly* reminding himself that he stood at the crossroads between faith in God and fear of people. He was always alert to his vulnerability to the fear of people. Likewise, if you have been in situations that have been physically threatening, you'd better be alert. It is a slippery slope between normal fear and an idolatrous fear of man. To stay on track, meditate on the Psalms with faith, and follow David's example.

> The LORD is the stronghold of my life—
>   of whom shall I be afraid?
> When evil men advance against me
>   to devour my flesh,
> when my enemies and my foes attack me,
>   they will stumble and fall. . . .
> Though war break out against me,

even then I will be confident.
One thing I ask of the LORD,
    this is what I seek:
that I may dwell in the house of the LORD
    all the days of my life,
to gaze upon the beauty of the LORD
    and to seek him in his temple. (Ps. 27:1–4)

If you can read this psalm and say that it expresses the desire of your heart, then your fear is not a sinful fear of man.

Janet: A Case Study

The best-known physical threat in contemporary culture is physical or sexual violence against women. Certainly women *and* men have been physically and sexually mistreated, but women tend to be more vulnerable and more frequently targeted.

Without question, the sexual violation of women leaves them more vulnerable to the fear of people. Their experience literally screams that people are more powerful than God. After all, if God is loving, why didn't he stop the oppressor?

Consider the logic of the book, *When Bad Things Happen to Good People.* It insists that tragedy forces us to make a decision: Do we believe that God is powerful *or* loving? The author does not believe that both are possible.

> [The author of the book of Job] is prepared to give up his belief . . . that God is all powerful. Bad things do happen to good people, but it is not God who wills it. God would like people to get what they deserve in life, but He cannot always arrange it. Forced to choose between a good God who is totally powerful, or a powerful God

who is not totally good, the author of the Book of Job chooses to believe in God's goodness.[1]

Either God is not loving, or God is not powerful, says Rabbi Kushner. Either way, God's true glory is quickly tainted by such thoughts. He becomes smaller in our minds. We no longer fear him appropriately. We only fear people who seem more powerful than ourselves.

If anyone had reason to fear people who seemed more powerful, it was Janet. The repeated sexual violation by her father and the violence of her brother were defining events in her life. But she has been working hard to move beyond the pains of her past. Over the past months Janet has read a number of popular Christian and secular books on self-esteem and self-love. They have all seemed to describe her perfectly. In fact, she has felt more understood by these books than she has by her own husband. She also confesses that these books have helped her understand herself better than the Bible ever did. Now, whenever she has a problem in her life, she traces it to "feeling bad about myself": "What I really need is to like myself. I have hated myself for so many years that it feels like a disease."

Such self-focus is understandable. Janet feels filled with shame, and self-loathing can be an expression of shame. But unless her self-examination is biblically guided, things will only get worse. Her present course is taking her away from people and making it impossible for her to grow in the fear of the Lord.

For example, Janet has been reluctant to come to church for the last two months. Her six-year-old son can be very active and demanding, and sometimes he creates problems in Sunday school. The teacher has been creative in finding ways to work with him, and

---

1   Harold S. Kushner, *When Bad Things Happen to Good People* (New York: Schocken, 1981), 43.

he is doing better now that she has assigned an adult to him full-time, but the teacher thought it would be helpful if Janet knew what was happening. After she mentioned some of his behaviors to Janet, Janet responded graciously but inwardly was mortified and angry. She was embarrassed that her son was singled out, and she took the teacher's comments as a personal attack on her mothering. "Now everyone thinks I'm a bad mother," she concluded.

For all Janet's pursuit of better self-esteem, her fear of man is growing. She avoids her son's Sunday school teacher, and she has begun to think (without evidence) that all the other women in the church are criticizing her behind her back. Other people—at least her perceptions of them—are controlling her more and more.

At this point, the main reason she comes to church at all is to see the assistant pastor. Recently she confessed to being infatuated with him. He had been pastorally attentive when Janet had some recent medical problems, and now Janet cannot stop thinking about him. She keeps thinking about an affair with him. She fantasizes about marriage. Sometimes she sanitizes the fantasy by marrying the pastor after her husband dies in a car accident.

She confessed these thoughts to her husband, and he responded well. He was hurt yet tried to be as helpful to her as possible. He tried to love her more. He struggled, however, when it became clear that there was nothing he could do to budge her fantasies. He gradually began to see that even though he could show grace and love to his wife, he couldn't change her heart. Janet had set up a person-idol in her life and was now controlled by it.

The Trail of the Fear of Man

What is going on in Janet's relationships with her abusers, the Sunday school teacher, and the assistant pastor? Why is she in various ways controlled by them? Isn't it a result of shame-fear, rejection-fear, and threat-fear?

Let's look at her situation more closely. Shame runs deep in Janet. She feels uncovered and defiled. She thinks that a relationship with her father and brother might help, so she longs for it. She reads the self-esteem literature and it describes worthlessness, the secular surface of shame, and she feels as if it describes her. She gets a negative report about her son and feels further exposed as unworthy. Every day she feels as if her walls of self-protection are being pulled down. She feels more and more vulnerable to being hurt by others. The shame is so intense that she thinks about physically hurting herself as a way to momentarily distract herself and find relief.

Do you remember that shame-fear can be a result of our own sin, the sins of those who victimize us, or both? Janet's shame is a result of both, and her responses to her shame reveal a confused interweaving of the two sources in her life. Janet needs the healing clarity of a biblical perspective, but so far it has eluded her.

A fairly straightforward issue in Janet's life is the shame from sin that is a result of her sexual fantasy about the assistant pastor and the way it has hurt her husband. She has confessed these and other sins probably hundreds of times, but she still feels unclean.

There are reasons why her sense of uncleanness persists. First, there is a part of Janet that wants to hold onto the fantasy relationship. Its benefits outweigh its disadvantages for her. For one thing, she wants to follow her own lusts; she likes this sin rather than hates it. It has become a comfortable way to cope with the fall-out from the sins of others, both real and perceived. A second, more subtle reason Janet does not feel forgiven from this sin is that she confuses the shame from her sin with the shame from her victimization. Janet actually believes that she is responsible for the sins of her brother and father, and this has shaped this part of her life as well.

How would you help Janet? The biblical response to the shame from Janet's own sin is to teach her repentance and a hatred of sin. Janet is not responsible for the sins of other people, but she is responsible for her own. The way to eliminate shame associated with sin is to *admit* sin, be confident that God forgives sin, and engage in battle against it.

Janet's shame from her sinful victimization is more difficult to resolve. Though the shame from her own sin is the deeper spiritual problem of the two, in many ways it is easier to cover. Such shame can be covered through a confession of sin, repentance, and faith in the finished work of Jesus, as we have seen. Shame from victimization can be more stubborn. Confession of sin cannot release it because the victim is not the guilty party. But that doesn't stop people from trying. "If I could just confess my sin better, then I could feel clean," they say.

In an effort to feel clean or covered, some victims have resorted to punishing themselves as if works of penance would miraculously cleanse and cover. They try to resolve things with God by cutting their bodies, being hopelessly depressed, ruining their marriage so they get what they think they deserve, or practicing some idiosyncratic forms of self-loathing. Of course, penance never covers or cleanses, but out of either ignorance or unbelief, many victims feel bereft of other options and they resort to penance again and again.

There is some of this going on in Janet. In the aftermath of being sinned against by her father and brother, she feels as if she has been naked all her life. She always feels unclean and defiled. No matter what she does, she still feels dirty. Her only explanation is that she must have caused her father and brother to sin against her. It must have been her fault. She must have seduced them in some way. Her seductive fantasy with the pastor is, in part, Janet's saying, "This is who I am; I am a seductive person who ruins lives." She also thinks that she is such a vile person that she deserves no blessings, such as a good husband. She deserves to be divorced from him; then he could marry someone who would be a better wife. She can't bring herself to have an actual affair, but perhaps the fantasy alone will give her husband the out that he needs.

Crazy thinking, isn't it? It is biblically unchecked thinking that has been intensified by her past. More specifically, it is *sinful* thinking because *her* interpretation of her past is taking precedence over God's interpretation. But it is also thinking that can be changed with a clear biblical structure.

A Biblical Structure to Overcome Shame and Threat

The biblical structure begins with bringing godly clarity to the experience of shame. Shame is something that we do to ourselves *and* is done to us. Now is the time for Janet to distinguish between the two forms. Perhaps Janet could read through examples of victimization-shame in Scripture: stories such as Dinah (Gen. 34:5), examples from Levitical laws (e.g., Lev. 11:24), and the defilement of the temple because of the presence of unclean men (Ps. 79). The clearest example is Jesus himself. He was sentenced to death in the most shameful manner possible—naked and on a cross. He felt shame, but he was innocent. He suffered the shame of others that was placed on him. This is the One on whom Janet must fix her eyes (Heb. 12:2). Then, instead of focusing on her works-righteous attempts to repay God for a sin that is not hers, she can focus her attention outside of herself, on who God is and what he says.

What is God's response to victims who have trusted in him? First, he understands their shame. This understanding is not an aloof, intellectual knowledge. God actually grieves over the victimization of his children, and he is doing something about it. We may not see the wheels of heaven turning, and Janet may not see them turning with regard to her specific victimization in her lifetime, but we know by faith that God does not abandon those who have been victimized (cf. Ps. 22).

God extends his compassion and his mighty, rescuing arm to take away shame. Jesus both experienced shame and took our shame on himself, so shame no longer defines us. In fact, by grace through faith, it is no longer part of us. Then, in an act that seems inconceivable, God goes a step further: he marries and exalts those who once were shamed.

> *Do not be afraid; you will not suffer shame.*
> *Do not fear disgrace; you will not be humiliated.*
> *You will forget the shame of your youth*
>   *and remember no more the reproach of your widowhood.*
> *For your Maker is your husband—*
>   *the LORD Almighty is his name—*
> *the Holy One of Israel is your Redeemer. (Isa. 54:4–5)*

Words of hope and delight to Janet? Probably not immediately. The thought of being married to the Most High might be more terrifying than wonderful to her. It is likely that if she has any evident fear of the Lord, it is a terror that seeks to avoid God rather than a robust reverence. It will be difficult for her to believe the extent of God's grace. She will constantly be looking at herself and her sense of unworthiness and filthiness, and she will try to hide from the Holy One.

But she must believe. She must believe in the words of Christ more than she believes in anything else. She must follow the principle: For every one look at myself I must take ten looks at Jesus. She must meditate on these loving promises from the mouth of God. If she thinks that she is beyond grace, she should be corrected.

Such thinking is based on the unbiblical assumption that our works can either keep us away from God or move us toward him. It is a denial of grace itself. It suggests that there is some righteous act she must perform in order to meet God halfway. This, however, has nothing to do with the gospel of Jesus. The gospel is *only* available to people who know they are unclean.

Janet's fear of being exposed (shame) stands alongside her fear of being attacked (threat). Having grown up in a home where there were unpredictable sexual assaults, Janet was always looking over her shoulder. She always felt as if "some catastrophe is going to happen to me—I feel like it is always just around the corner." She felt small, and she felt as if she lived among people who were very powerful. She had a clear profession of faith, but the day-in and day-out process of trusting in the loving and almighty hand of God was absent. When people are large, God will be small.

One might think that an extensive study of the sovereign power of God would help Janet deal with this particular aspect of her fear of people. However, pictures of an enthroned God will not speak deeply to this fear of attack. Janet must know that the sovereign God is *good*. Chances are that she believes that God reigns over all things, but that his love toward her is small. She has succumbed to Satan's suggestions that God is not really for his people. Only persistent meditation on the cross of Christ is sufficient to allay this fear. Then she will know that there is no person capable of thwarting God's good purposes in her life.

With other people so large in her life, Janet most likely would feel very sensitive to rejection, and, indeed, she did. If there ever was a leaky love cup looking to be filled with acceptance, it was she. She felt as if she needed the constant affirmation and praise of her husband. She needed her brother and father to give her the relationship she had never had with them. She needed to be understood, and she resented having to get that from books rather than from women in the church. She needed to be perceived as a good mother. And she needed closeness from other men. But these things never filled her. She was always looking for more.

Please understand that *anyone* who has gone through Janet's experiences would feel a certain sense of emptiness. The loss of good relationships with family members is grievous, and the desire to have good relationships is strong. It is not this desire that constitutes the fear of people. It is when desires are elevated to demands that there are detectable people-idols in our lives. It is when desires become demands that we are more concerned about *our* desires than the glory of God.

In Janet, desire, indeed, has grown into demand that feels like need. She does not believe that God can be trusted with her life, and so she has turned to other people for safety and security. The way out for her is to confess that she has been busy needing other people for her own faithless purposes. She can instead seek to love other people out of the love and security she enjoys in Christ, in a desire to glorify him. Then, instead of defining herself exclusively as *needy*, she could practice one of the dominant shapes that God gives us: we are servants of the Most High God who are called to love more than need.

Does this sound like I am being too hard on Janet? I hope not. The story of the Old Testament is one in which God condemns injustice and oppression; he is filled with compassion for the victim. Half of the Psalms meditate on this theme. So all counsel given Janet must be filled with compassion for her and anger over the injustices she suffered. Otherwise, it is not biblical counsel.

Does it sound like I am excusing Janet's sin? I hope not. Such a tragic history does not mean that we ignore sin in Janet's life. To do that would mean that her victimization problem is deeper than her sin problem, and the truth is that there is nothing deeper than our own sinfulness. Also, to ignore Janet's sin would be to further victimize her. It would keep her from knowing true freedom from guilt, the joy of forgiveness, and the greatness of God's love.

The problem with many Christian books on victimization is that they never really take us out of ourselves and allow us to put our hope in Christ alone. Instead, they seem to leave us trapped in pain. Yet the Christian view of victimization is consistently God-centered, and this has been the goal in counseling Janet. Biblical guidance starts with hearing about God's great compassion. It proceeds to examine our own hearts so that we can grow in obedience to Christ, and it ends with trusting that our God is the almighty God who is just and loving.

Can a history of victimization intensify our inclination to fear people? There is no question that it can make some people more susceptible. But such a history cannot force us into the fear of man, nor can it prevent us from leaving that fear behind.

The Choice Before Us

Jeremiah 17 is the classic biblical text on the fear of man. It reduces the decisions of life to two options: Will you trust in man or will you trust in the Lord?

> *Cursed is the one who trusts in man,*
> *   who depends on flesh for his strength*
> *   and whose heart turns away from the LORD.*
> *He will be like a bush in the wastelands;*
> *   he will not see prosperity when it comes.*
> *He will dwell in the parched places of the desert,*
> *   in a salt land where no one lives.*
> *But blessed is the man who trusts in the LORD,*

whose confidence is in him.
He will be like a tree planted by the water
that sends out its roots by the stream.
It does not fear when the heat comes;
its leaves are always green.
It has no worries in a year of drought
and never fails to bear fruit. (Jer. 17:5–8)

The Old Testament indicates that we stand at the crossroads between fear of others and fear of God. The road leading to the fear of man may be expressed in terms of favoritism, wanting others to think well of you, fearing exposure by them, or being overwhelmed by their perceived physical power. When these fears are not combated with the fear of the Lord, the consequences can be devastating. But when God is given his rightful place in our lives, old bonds can be shattered.

For Further Thought

Consider meditating on another section of Scripture. When Jesus was sending out the disciples to call others into the kingdom, he reminded them that they would encounter a number of problems. People would reject them, they would be turned over to town councils for public flogging, and their ministry would be divisive, thus angering even more people. In other words, the disciples would be tempted to fear people. As a result, Jesus sent them off saying, "Do not be afraid of those who kill the body but cannot kill the soul. Rather, be afraid of the One who can destroy both soul and body in hell" (Matt. 10:28).

Jesus' exhortation talked specifically about the fear of physical threats, similar to the ones that faced Abraham. But he is taking the worst scenario—being killed—and saying that even the threat of death should not cause the disciples to fear other people. If such a severe threat could be countered with the fear of the Lord, then threats such as rejection would not be lethal blows. Don't forget, the disciples were just like us. They wanted people to like them. Therefore, friends and other people within Israel could be just as dangerous as enemies who wanted to kill.

Think about Jesus' exhortation: "Do not be afraid of those who kill the body but cannot kill the soul. Rather, be afraid of the One who can destroy both soul and body in hell." Can you feel its liberating force? There is something about the power of God, not to mention the thought of hell, that cuts through the painful introspection associated with the fear of others.

CHAPTER

"THE WORLD WANTS ME TO FEAR PEOPLE"

Individualism, at first, only saps the virtues of public life; but, in the long run, it attacks and destroys all others, and is at length absorbed in downright selfishness. Selfishness is a vice as old as the world . . . individualism is of democratic origin.

—Alexis De Tocqueville

WE do not need to be persuaded or manipulated to put our hope in people more than in God. Like a child's temper tantrum, this is not a behavior that needs to be observed or learned. Fear of man is something we do naturally. Since the Fall, it is a human instinct. But, sadly, our hearts have a partner in crime. The world and its sub-biblical assumptions aggravate our tendency to fear or reverence others.

STEP 3 *Identify where your fear of man has been intensified by the assumptions of the world.*

This should come as no surprise. The Bible warns that there is a quiet, sub-biblical pattern to the world that begs us to conform to it. The Lord constantly warned Old Testament Israel that the world around them, with its idolatrous practices, was a dangerous threat. The early church, too, was influenced by the world. The Jewish culture kept pulling the gospel message into works-righteousness and legalism (Col. 2). Certainly, our era is no different from every other time in the history of God's people. The world tempts our hearts to live for the approval of others, too.

How does the world—our "corporate flesh"[1]—encourage the fear of man? Consider a few examples. One common observation about our world is that we live in a culture of victimization. It is always the other person's fault. You are responsible for my actions. We even blame other people for our culture of victimization: the lawyers did it. They victimized us into the culture of victimization.

Notice the implications of such blame-shifting. We are saying that other people control our behavior. Isn't that the fear of man? If we are chronic victims, we are shifting the locus of control from ourselves to others. We are saying that other people made us do it. Of course, there *is* real victimization in this world, but nearly everyone acknowledges that we have also fostered an entirely new—and dubious—breed of victims.

The emphasis on self-esteem also contributes to the fear of man. For example, even though most self-esteem books indicate that it is something you can develop by yourself, almost all the books also say that one of the best ways to raise your self-esteem is to achieve some successes (which are then compared to what *others* do) or to surround yourself with people who affirm you (which leaves you dependent on *their* opinion). If you have money, your self-esteem can be inflated by a warm, empathic therapist.

1 Richard Lovelace, *Renewal as a Way of Life* (Downers Grove, Ill.: InterVarsity Press, 1985), 86.

There are quiet, unbiblical assumptions in our culture that shape our thinking and dictate the questions we ask. Sometimes we call this *the world,* as in "the world, the flesh, and the Devil." These assumptions even affect our interpretations of the Bible. For example, since our culture has taught us to think individually rather than corporately, we are prone to think about *me* rather than *us.* Our interpretation of "do not give the devil a foothold" (Eph. 6:27) is a classic illustration. This passage is consistently applied to the individual. That is, if you are sinfully angry, Satan will have some sort of control in your life. Although this may be true, the passage is speaking in the context of the *church.* Ephesians is about unity in the *church.* The foothold refers to Satan's divisive influence in the body of Christ rather than Satan possessing an individual. The treatment is to hotly pursue unity in the church.

No matter how biblical we think we are, it is impossible to avoid being affected by these assumptions. Worldly presuppositions are in the air we breathe.

Have you ever been in big-city smog? I remember the first time I drove toward Los Angeles. It was literally enveloped in a bubble of smog. Yet once I was in Los Angeles, the smog seemed to disappear. I would look up in the sky and it appeared perfectly blue. As long as there was no background, such as mountains, the air looked crystal clear. This is the nature of worldly assumptions. When you are surrounded by them, you don't see them.

Our goal in this chapter is to take a moment and notice the smog that surrounds us. We need to see that in our battle against being controlled by other people, we are fighting not only our own hearts, but the trends in our culture.

Some Modern Assumptions

Significant cultural changes started in the late 1700s and early

1800s. Before this, people believed that there was a preordained, divine structure to the world. Everybody and everything had its place. If you were born into a certain class, family, or trade, your life was mapped out for you. "I am an Englishman, I am a member of St. Anne's parish, I am a farmer, and I am the second son of Charles." Such was your identity. There was no need for vocational and religious decisions; they had already been made for you. There were few identity crises when everyone knew who and what they were "supposed" to be. Consequently, problems with self-esteem rarely surfaced. (This is not to say that the culture did not have other problems; simply that questions about identity and personhood were configured differently.)

The rise of a middle class changed much of that thinking, however. Life roles were no longer set in stone. New radical thoughts about one's life and identity—and the possibilities that had previously gone unexplored—arose when the middle class flexed its muscles in the French Revolution (1789). This event was a political marker for something much deeper that was taking place. With the blurring of distinctions between father and son, peasant and nobleman, and without clear biblical thinking shaping the new social structure, a new worldview arose that placed much more value on individual growth, *personal* identity, and the immense possibilities of the person without linking it to a submission to divine authority. It was the rise of Western culture as we know it today, and it has rightly been called the rise of the cult of the self.

Assumptions About God

God was still part of this culture. In fact, most people, both then and now, would say that God exists and that the soul is immortal. That sounds pretty good—a little basic, perhaps, with no explicit statement about Jesus, but it seems essentially Christian.

But jump to the present for a moment. How do you react to a recent poll indicating that the vast majority of Americans believe in God, an afterlife, and even the existence of angels? Are you encouraged to think that America is a Christian country? Or are you somewhat suspicious, left wanting to ask a few more questions? You can probably guess my reaction. We live in a time when there is a resurgence of God-talk and spiritual language, but conversations rarely get to the thing of "first importance: that Christ died for our sins according to the Scriptures, that he was buried, that he was raised on the third day according to the Scriptures, and that he appeared to Peter and then to the Twelve" (1 Cor. 15:3–5).

The last two centuries have introduced God language that sounds fine but is divorced from biblical content. For example, the French philosopher Rousseau talked about God, but he found his god in nature. His god was all peace and goodness, and he moved people to a *feeling* of worship. Rousseau shifted the focus from objective revelation (the Bible) to subjective experience (feelings), from other people to the inner life, and from loving God and neighbor to loving self.

Can you see in this the outline for modern culture—and ourselves? The authority of feelings and the language of spirituality without the content—these are the assumptions of our culture.

Of course, these assumptions can't continue for long before the real implications about God come to the surface. The quiet revolution has been committed to exalting ourselves and rendering God as less than holy and sovereign. A speech by Ralph Waldo Emerson made this all too clear.

> Divine as the life of Jesus is, what an outrage to represent it as tantamount to the Universe! To seize one accidental good man that happened to exist somewhere at some time and say to the new-

born soul, "Behold thy pattern ... go into the harness of that past individual, assume his manners, speak his speech,"—this is the madness of Christendom. ... I turn my back on these usurpers. *The soul always believes in itself.*[2]

The supreme interest has become the self. Not God, not you, but *me.*

Can you see connections between then and now? Our culture has embraced a "God as we understand him" who is known by way of an inner journey. "GodDependency is . . . relying on your own understanding of what a loving God is and does for you."[3] "There are myriad approaches to both prayer and meditation. No way is the right way. ... The real thing is the actual experience of God. ... Spiritual growth comes through deepening insight into my being."[4] These are the fruits of a pluralistic, you-do-your-thing-and-I-do-mine culture. "I have my version of God, and you have your version of God." The only immoral act in such a culture is to say that your version of God is superior to anyone else's.

As these assumptions have gained more acceptance, there has been an unprecedented increase in depression and an astonishing rise in the number of people who confess to rage against God. There is a grass-roots cry from people who are demanding both answers and "rights" from God. Then, in perhaps the zenith of self-exaltation, some clergy and counselors actually encourage such angry people to "forgive God."

---

2 Ralph Waldo Emerson, *The Journals and Miscellaneous Notebooks, VII: 1838–42,* ed. A. W. Plumstead and H. Hayford (Cambridge, Mass.: Harvard University Press, 1969), 254.

3 Lynne Bundesen, *GodDependency* (New York: Crossway, 1989), 59.

4 John Bradshaw, *Bradshaw On: The Family* (Deerfield Beach, Fla.: Health Communications, 1988), 234, 236.

Can you see how these assumptions influence the fear of man? Anything that erodes the fear of God will intensify the fear of man.

Assumptions About Ourselves

If our culture is misguided in its understanding of God, then it will be misguided in its understanding of people who are made in his image. And this, indeed, is what we are witnessing in the assumptions about human nature that are now routinely made. Let's look at some of them.

We are morally good. The air we breathe says that evil does not exist within us—it exists outside us. The momentum behind this began with the nineteenth-century belief that we could find human innocence and innate moral beauty in those who were uncorrupted by civilization, such as children. The child, according to Schlegel, was "the clear mirror in which we gaze upon the secrets of divine love."[5]

Does this sound familiar? Have you heard of the "child within"? It is thought to be the innocent essence that exists within us all. With such a spiritual core, people could look to themselves for divinity and revelation. Samuel Coleridge, in *Biographia Literaria* (1817), wrote: "We begin with the I KNOW MYSELF, in order to end with the absolute I AM. We proceed from the SELF, in order to lose and find all self in GOD." There was no longer any need to look outside the self—either to God or other people—for what is true. Truth is found in the person.

How modern! These assumptions can be found in counseling offices where Christians are nonchalant about forgiveness of sin yet zealous about personal needs. Or they can be found on most talk shows where self-revelation is lavishly indulged and glorified.

5 *An Anthology of Modern Philosophy*, comp. D. S. Robinson (New York: Thomas Crowell, 1931), 508.

Consider Nathaniel Branden's comments from *Honoring the Self,* a book praised in Melody Beattie's best seller, *Codependent No More.*

> To honor the self is to be in love with our own life, in love with our possibilities for growth and for the experiencing of joy, in love with the process of discovery and exploring our distinctively human potentialities. Thus we can begin to see that to honor the self is to practice selfishness in the highest, noblest, and the least understood sense of the word. And this, I shall argue, requires enormous independence, courage, and integrity.[6]

These words would not have been written prior to the 1800s. Or, if they had been, they would have been condemned as the words of a heretic. Today, they are the words of the person on the street. They are a foundational cultural assumption: we are good people who must love ourselves in order to be healthy.

"Love your neighbor as yourself" (Matt. 19:19) is considered the biblical proof text (for those who need one). When interpreted through cultural spectacles, this verse means that we must love ourselves in order to love other people. But in reality the passage doesn't even suggest such an interpretation. Jesus spoke these words to a rich young man who clearly loved himself and his possessions *too much.* There is only one command in the passage, and it is "love your neighbor." Nobody, including the writers of Scripture, could have dreamed that this passage taught self-love. It took some cultural changes to reinterpret it and turn our eyes inward.

The Bible assumes that we have more than enough self-concern.

6 Nathaniel Branden, *Honoring the Self: Personal Integrity and the Heroic Potentials of Human Nature* (Boston: Houghton Mifflin, 1983), 4.

We dress ourselves. We get depressed when things don't go our way. We can be consumed with what someone thinks about us. But cultural assumptions have blinded us. We no longer see the smog we live in. So pastors of many growing churches preach almost weekly about healthy self-esteem, as if it were taught on every page of Scripture. Too many Christians never see that self-love comes out of a culture that prizes the individual over the community and then reads that basic principle into the pages of Scripture. The Bible, however, rightly understood, asks the question, "Why are you so concerned about yourself?" Furthermore, it indicates that our culture's proposed cure—increased self-love—is actually the disease. If we fail to recognize the reality and depth of our sin problem, God will become less important, and people will become more important.

Emotions are the way to truth. If I am a good person who occasionally does bad things, then it follows that what I feel is also generally good. "Feeling is all," said Faust. Feelings have become the inarticulate mutterings of the divine soul: to be morally upright is to do whatever your heart inspires you to do. When following inner impulses, this assumption declares, we can do no wrong.

"God told me to marry John," said Mary. She looked ecstatic, and the pastor was hoping to share her happiness.

"Please, tell me a little about him."

"Well, he isn't a Christian yet. In fact, he refuses to even come to church, but I know that he will someday."

"Mary, how do you know that you should marry him? How did God tell you?"

"Pastor, I just feel it. I know it's right."

The conversation is now over. Mary has just appealed to the highest authority—her feelings. In two years, she will appeal to this authority again.

"Pastor, I don't believe that God wants me to stay in an unhappy relationship, and I have been unhappy with John for the past year. He won't go to any church with me, he is consumed with work and sports, and we are almost never together sexually. I just don't feel like I love him anymore. So, I have decided to divorce."

Even in worship services, the goal for many is that people *feel* something. Schleiermacher, a German theologian of the 1800s, made this the essence of religion. Theology for him was nothing more than religious feelings made articulate. "Religion," he said, "is a feeling of absolute dependence."[7] Although Schleiermacher was extreme in his views, aren't they recognizable today? Have you watched the faith healers? Have you heard preachers who hope to create an aesthetic response to the sermon? The church's emphasis on emotion may be more dependent on cultural traditions than on Scripture.

It is not just happy emotions that are our focus. Since emotions in general are thought to be our main source of truth, we also tend to be especially interested in our pain. Orthodox Christian thought has always talked about suffering, but in the context of sanctification, not self-improvement. The goal is the glory of Christ. This is very different from saying that emotions are the tools that allow us to be fully aware of our needs. It is also contrary to the idea that the suppression of emotions is one of the cardinal sins of our culture, and only increased acceptance of feelings will promote our well-being.

Certainly, the Psalms encourage us to speak honestly to God in our suffering, but today we are told to "embrace legitimate suffering" and "enter into grief." Such interest in personal pain tends to drive us into ourselves rather than outward to a biblical under-

---

7 *On Religion: Speeches to Its Cultured Despisers* (New York: Harper & Row, 1965), 106.

standing of God, *his* grief, and heavenly things rather than earthly. "Get in touch with your feelings," is a sound-bite from the 1800s. It just took a while to catch on.

This exaltation of feelings has changed the way we think. For example, I just heard a sermon that offered a new, romanticized purpose for prayer. "The purpose of prayer," began the preacher, "is an awareness of the presence of God." I gleaned helpful applications from the sermon, but his lead statement was wrong. The awareness of God's presence is not the purpose of prayer. The preacher was appealing to experience junkies who wanted an emotional boost out of worship, sermons, and prayer.

There was a time in my own life when I would "practice the presence of God"; then, when I felt his presence, I would pray. All went well until the day I didn't feel his presence. I waited for hours, filled with tears, but I never felt The Presence. I tried to pray but I felt that both I and my prayers were in a hermetically sealed room. The Presence finally came the next day when I was asking for counsel from a good friend. His comment was simply this: "Why didn't you just pray by faith?" He taught me one of the most important lessons of prayer: that prayer depended on God and his promises, not my own quixotic emotions.

Keep looking around. You can find the exaltation of feelings everywhere. For example, you can find it in the way we have revised our idea of shame. Shame was originally viewed as the result of a problem between God and ourselves. Now it is reduced to whatever prevents us from *feeling* good about ourselves.

Listen for the popular question at Bible studies, "What do *you feel* about this passage?" Is it possible that our feelings are often more important to us than faith? Too often, if our faith is weak, we don't see it as a serious problem. It is only when our feelings are distressing that we decide to ask others for help and prayer.

Throughout the history of the church, emotions were always viewed with suspicion because they could vacillate so wildly. Now they are praised. Too often they are the standards by which we make judgments.

When feelings become more important than faith, people will become more important, and God will become less important.

All people are spiritual. It is against this backdrop that we encounter another cultural assumption about the need for more spirituality. Spirituality, however, has been reduced to a *feeling* of the infinite, an inarticulate ecstasy before the wonders of the self or nature, or an experience of the ineffable. Modern spirituality has no hell, no doctrine, no substance. It is about feeling.

Choreographer Todd Williams says that, in his latest work, he is talking about "becoming one with the infinite. By realizing that your soul is a perfect reflection of God or cosmic consciousness, you're able to unite your soul with that consciousness."[8]

Over a hundred and fifty years ago, the Danish philosopher Kierkegaard (1813–55) was observing the same thing. He noticed that many people were going to church but "the thing of becoming and being a Christian is now a triviality."

> What does it mean that all these thousands call themselves Christians as a matter of course? These many, many men of whom the greater part, so far as one can judge, live in categories quite foreign to Christianity! Anyone can convince himself of it by the simplest of observations. People who perhaps never once enter church, never think about God, never mention his name except in oaths! People upon whom it has never dawned that they might have any obligation to God. . . . At the bottom of this there must be a

8 *Los Angeles Times,* July 29, 1995, F2.

tremendous confusion, a frightful illusion, there surely can be no doubt.[9]

Kierkegaard sounds like a prophet for our age. The baby-boomers are going back to church, but sometimes it doesn't seem as if the kingdom is forcefully advancing.

Alcoholics Anonymous (AA) is another example. When AA founder Bill Wilson was in the hospital, drying out from another drunken spree, he saw a bright light, which he interpreted as a religious experience. He later said that this religious experience was essential to his sobriety. But the religious experience was totally divorced from a personal God. Instead, "spiritual" simply meant ineffable, a feeling of wholeness and wonder.

Today you can be spiritual, it would seem, if you believe in your left shoe.

➤ "I take what I want of the Bible and the church and leave the rest."

➤ "[AA] meetings are about finding spiritual power."

➤ "I still have problems with the idea of a Christian God up there. … I think of God as the Universe with its own sense of good."

Spirituality is back in style. In an age when technology is exploding, we still know that there is mystery. People want to retain a sense of wonder in their lives. To put it more biblically, the knowledge of God cannot be denied; it can only be distorted.

When God and spirituality are reduced to *our* standards or our feelings, God will never be to us the awesome Holy One of Israel. With God reduced in our eyes, a fear of people will thrive.

9 Soren Kierkegaard, *The Point of View for My Work as an Author: A Report to History* (New York: Harper & Row, 1962), 74.

Psychology: The Caretaker of Cultural Assumptions

American psychology has become the official caretaker of these modern assumptions. It has nurtured the person-as-good, the emphasis on emotions, and the importance of spirituality. It has also developed a related theme: the person-as-psychologically-needy.

Notice Freud's influence on this. Although he didn't specifically use the word "need," he has been cited as the father of "the need for sexual expression" and "the need for permissive parents." He talked about "instincts" (needs) which clamor for expression, and he claimed that if these instincts are not satisfied, adult neurosis is the result.

The true popularizer of the concept of psychological needs was Abraham Maslow. His self-actualization theory suggested that we have, at birth, a hierarchy of needs. According to Maslow, the most basic needs are biological and safety needs. When these needs are met, we can move up to satisfy the basic psychological needs: the need for belonging and love, the need for esteem from other people, and the need for self-esteem.

> What makes people neurotic? My answer . . . was, in brief, that neurosis seemed at its core, and in its beginning, to be a deficiency disease: that it was born out of being deprived of certain satisfactions which I called needs in the same sense that water and amino acids and calcium are needs, namely that their absence produces illness. Most neuroses involved . . . ungratified wishes for safety, for belongingness and identification, for close love relationships and for respect and prestige.[10]

Freud and Maslow each think about needs (drives) differently, but they agree on three basic points: psychological needs exist, they

10 Abraham Maslow, *Toward a Psychology of Being* (New York: Van Nostrand, 1968), 21.

are an essential part of being human, and unmet needs will result in some kind of personal pathology. To these essentials can be added one further characteristic of psychological need or deficit theories: they are distinctly American. Need theories can thrive only in a context where the emphasis is on the individual rather than the community and where consumption is a way of life. If you ask most Asians or Africans about their psychological needs, they will not even understand the question!

This rise of psychological needs was inevitable: If you exalt the individual and make emotions the path to truth, then whatever you feel most strongly will be considered both good and *necessary* for growth. Whatever you feel most strongly are seen as your God-given needs. That is why the unpardonable sin in today's culture is to either "deny" or suppress your emotions. Emotions point to needs, and to deny your needs is to deny something God-given and God-like.

Can you hear the way our culture *encourages* the fear of man? "Needs" or "rights" lead irresistibly into fear of man. We've seen that whatever you think you need, you come to fear. If you "need" love (to feel okay about yourself), you will soon be controlled by the one who dispenses love. You are also saying that without that person's love you will be spiritually handicapped, unable to give love to others. With this kind of spiritually crippling logic bearing bad fruit everywhere, it is no wonder that even psychologists are calling for a reformation in our culture's fundamental assumptions.

Psychologists, however, have made their own contribution to this. While they have accurately noted that people with low self-esteem put too much hope in others and fear people, their therapy does not liberate. Notice what they offer: therapeutic acceptance, unconditional love, and constant affirmation. In other words, "Don't believe what other people have said about you, and don't even believe your own negative self-reports; instead, believe what *I* say." Such therapy rehabilitates fear of man rather than eliminating it. It just feels a little better because the client is putting hope in someone who is affirming rather than accusing.

The Influence of Christian Psychology

Meanwhile, the Christian church has been listening to all that the world has been saying. Many pastors and church leaders have detected the unbiblical assumptions and have tried to expose them. However, the most popular response has been to assimilate the world's ideas with minor modifications. For example, a number-one best seller in the Christian book market made this "needs" assumption central to its understanding of the person. Its view of the person is similar to a cup—an empty, passive vessel waiting to be filled. The authors say,

> [There is a] God-given need to be loved that is born into every human infant. It is a legitimate need that must be met from cradle to grave. If children are deprived of love—if that primal need for love is not met—they carry the scars for life.[11]

If our needs cup is filled with the love of others, we are happy. If our cup is empty or only half full, we will be plagued with bad feelings.

Consider this quotation closely. It expresses an assumption held by scores of other Christian writers; it is our unexamined theology. And it *sounds* right. I have already confessed that I have felt needy and empty when I'm not loved the way I would like—or the way I "need." But just because I feel a "need" to be loved doesn't mean

11 Robert Hemfelt, Frank Minirth, and Paul Meier, *Love Is a Choice* (Nashville: Nelson, 1989), 34.

that this desire is really a "God-given need," a "legitimate need," or a "primal need." Perhaps what I am calling "need" is really disappointment or grief, or perhaps it is my demandingness and lust.

There really are certain God-given needs, but it will take a little more biblical investigation to sort them out. (We will do this in chapter 9.) At this point we can simply say that a discussion about needs is more complex than it first appears. It is possible that our present-day discussion about needs might be framed more by secular psychological theories than by Scripture.

If this is so, we should be careful about saying, "Jesus meets all our needs." At first, this has a plausible biblical ring to it. Christ *is* a friend; God *is* a loving Father; Christians *do* experience a sense of meaningfulness and confidence in knowing God's love. It makes Christ the answer to our problems. Yet if our use of the term "needs" is ambiguous, and its range of meaning extends all the way to selfish desires, then there will be some situations where we should say that Jesus does not intend to meet our needs, but that he intends to change our needs.[12]

The Emerging Backlash

One more thing has happened in this brief history of psychological needs. Currently, this popular and widely assumed view of the person is being questioned seriously in secular circles. People are coming to see that an absorption with neediness and emptiness is "unhealthy," both for individuals and society. For example, some in the popular press have criticized need theories as the theoretical justification for the rampant selfism and chronic victimhood of our culture. They see the implications: If human beings are truly in the

12 See Welch, "Who Are We? Needs, Longings, and the Image of God in Man," *The Journal of Biblical Counseling,* 13 (1994): 25–38.

shape of a cup, then we are passive recipients rather than active interpreters and responsible actors in our world. The blame never rests with ourselves, because all pathology is a result of deficits forged in past relationships. At the very least, suggest some in the media, this creates chaos in the justice system. "It will not be long, at this rate, before the mandatory sentence for a crime of violence is a hug and a good cry."[13]

The academic press is also challenging the idea that the modern person should be defined as an empty cup. In a significant article in the *American Psychologist,* Philip Cushman argued that the empty self is a dangerous product of a culture that wants to be filled, both psychically and materially.[14] The culprits, according to psychologist Cushman, are the psychological profession and the advertising industry. Both attempt to create a sense of need in order to sell products. Furthermore, the psychological selling of needs has led to a generation of empty, fragile, depressed individuals.

Historian and philosopher Christopher Lasch echoes these concerns.

> The contemporary climate is therapeutic, not religious. People today hunger not for personal salvation, let alone for the restoration of an earlier golden age, but for a feeling, the momentary illusion, of personal well-being, health, and psychic security.[15]

We live in a fascinating time. Parts of the church have been mesmerized by worldly assumptions, and these assumptions have intensified our problem with the fear of man. The world itself,

13 *The Economist,* February 26, 1994, 15.
14 Philip Cushman, "Why the Self Is Empty," *American Psychologist* (May 1990), 599.
15 Christopher Lasch, *The Culture of Narcissism* (New York: Norton, 1978), 7.

however, is challenging these same assumptions. It wants to see the demise of the leaky love cup, and it wants to reconsider its doctrine of neediness, but it has no satisfactory alternatives.

In other words, it is an ideal time for us to develop clear, meaningful, biblical teaching on who we are and how we can avoid being controlled by the things we feel we need.

For Further Thought

This chapter briefly reviews the history of some of our present cultural assumptions. It suggests that these assumptions have infected the church: the self as more important than community, the self as good, the exaltation of feelings and needs, and spirituality that is divorced from the death and resurrection of Jesus and a lifestyle of faith and obedience. Take some time to consider how these assumptions may have quietly influenced your own life.

1. Where do you find the assumptions of the world (in literature, art, movies, conversations)? Consider browsing through the self-help or psychology section of your local bookstore.

2. Where do you see these assumptions in you? Remember, these assumptions might not agree with your official theology, but they might be revealed in the way you live.

3. Ask missionaries from your church about what they see in the American church, not just the foreign church.

PART TWO   *Overcoming Fear of Others*

Part Two will explore the biblical ideas that will help you take the following steps to be free from the fear of man:

➤ Step 4: Understand and grow in the fear of the Lord. The person who fears God will fear nothing else.

➤ Step 5: Examine where your desires have been too big. When we fear people, people are big, our desires are even bigger, and God is small.

➤ Step 6: Rejoice that God has covered your shame, protected you from danger, and accepted you. He has filled you with his love.

➤ Step 7: Need other people less, love other people more. Out of obedience to Christ, and as a response to his love toward you, pursue others in love.

CHAPTER 6

KNOW THE FEAR
OF THE LORD

He will be the sure foundation for your times, a rich store of salvation and wisdom and knowledge; the fear of the Lord is the key to this treasure. —*Isaiah 33:6*

ALL experiences of the fear of man share at least one common feature: people are big. They have grown to idolatrous proportions in our lives. They control us. Since there is no room in our hearts to worship both God and people, whenever people are big, God is not. Therefore, the first task in escaping the snare of the fear of man is to know that *God* is awesome and glorious, not other people.

This clicked for me one Sunday while I was sitting in church. It was family month. Each Sunday for the month of February a different family would speak to the church about their family devotions. All the families were very edifying and, of course, horribly convicting, but the Schmurrs gave me a revelation. Roger Schmurr said that one of the things he tried to do during family devotions was talk about God.

That was it. That was my revelation.

Let me explain. As a counselor I live in a "how to" world. A depressed person talks with me because he or she wants to know how to get rid of depression. Couples don't feel any romance in their relationship. They want to know how to have that spark again. Sometimes, I confess, I speak more about the "how to" than about God.

I have two children who have brought home great Sunday school materials. Typically, I would read these papers on Sunday afternoon. They were always very helpful, full of biblical principles and their application. Lots of good "how to's." There were edifying stories of children who felt rejected by their friends and how Jesus could help them love those who were mean. I remember one on cheating that was especially good. But they rarely talked about God.

Don't get me wrong. I think that the application of Scripture to the details of our lives is great. My observation, however, is that these principles are not always embedded in the fear of the Lord. The result is that our goal can be self-improvement rather than the glory of the Holy God.

We need more sermons that leave us trembling.

STEP 4   *Understand and grow in the fear of the Lord. The person who fears God will fear nothing else.*

What Is the Fear of the Lord?

Please don't think only of terror when you think of the fear of the Lord. The fear of the Lord, like the fear of people, includes a spectrum of attitudes. On one side, the fear of the Lord does indeed mean a terror of God (threat-fear). We are unclean people, and we appear before the almighty God who is morally pure. We are rightly ashamed before him, and punishment would be completely just. Terror is our natural and appropriate response. Such fear shrinks back from God. It wants to avoid him as much as possible.

No one is excluded from this fear, Christians or non-Christians. For Christians whose eyes have been opened to God's great love, this fear is fading. For non-Christians such fear is ever-present. The reason you don't hear people talking about it is that it tends to come out in "free-floating anxiety," low self-esteem, and a host of other modern maladies that have lost sight of their God-ward roots. But this fear will not be camouflaged forever. The day is coming when everyone will bow before God in the fear of the Lord.

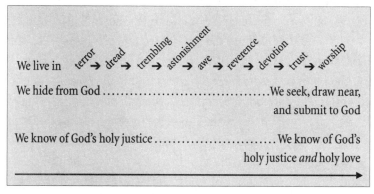

Figure 1. The Fear of the Lord: A Continuum

But this is only one end of the fear of the Lord. At the other end of the spectrum is a fear reserved exclusively for those who have put their faith in Jesus Christ. This fear of the Lord means *reverent submission that leads to obedience,* and it is interchangeable with "worship," "rely on," "trust," and "hope in." Like terror, it includes a knowledge of our sinfulness and God's moral purity, and it includes a clear-eyed knowledge of God's justice and his anger against sin. But this worship-fear also knows God's great forgiveness, mercy, and love. It knows that because of God's eternal plan, Jesus humbled himself by dying on a cross to redeem his enemies from slavery and death. It knows that, in our relationship with God, he always says "I love you" first. This knowledge draws us closer to God rather than causing us to flee. It causes us to submit gladly to his lordship and delight in obedience. This kind of robust fear is the pinnacle of our response to God.

Knowing the difference between these two fears clarifies why Scripture can say "There is no fear in love" (1 John 4:18) while simultaneously demanding the fear of the Lord. The Bible teaches that God's people are no longer driven by terror-fear, or fear that has to do with punishment. Instead, we are blessed with worship-fear, the reverential awe motivated more by love and the honor that is due him.

Why does the Bible use the same word for both responses? The biblical context always clarifies which kind of fear it is referring to, but the point is that both fears have something very important in common. They are both responses to the fact that the Holy One of Israel reigns over all the earth. This is the message of the Bible, and it is the essence of the fear of the Lord.

To appreciate the magnitude of this message, you should understand the biblical meaning of "holy." Holy can be defined as "separate," "set apart," "distinct," or "uncontaminated." In reference to God, "holy" means that he is different from us. None of his attributes can be understood by comparison to his creatures. His love and justice are above us; they are holy. His power is that of the Almighty; it can be compared to no one else's. His moral character is peerless; he alone is righteous.

Holiness is not one of many attributes of God. It is his essential nature and seen in all his qualities. His wisdom is a holy wisdom. His beauty a holy beauty. His majesty, a holy majesty. His holiness "adds glory, luster and harmony to all his other perfections."[1]

---

1 John M'Clintock and James Strong, "Holiness," *Cyclopedia of Biblical, Theological and Ecclesiastical Literature* (New York: Harper, 1872), 4:298.

"To whom will you compare me? Or who is my equal?" says the Holy One. (Isa. 40:25)

Your ways, O God, are holy. What god is so great as our God? (Ps. 77:13)

For I am God, and not man—the Holy One among you. (Hos. 11:9)

Some have called this "otherness," this holiness, of God his transcendence. God is exalted *above* his people. He lives in a high and lofty place (Isa. 57:15). His judgment and mercy are above us, they are ultimately incomprehensible. As a result, we don't use a reigning king or queen as our template for knowing God. To say that the *Holy* God reigns makes it impossible to use earthly kings as the model. The Holy God is unique, greater, and of a different kind than earthly kings. The Holy God is the original; the most glorious of earthly kings are only a dim reflection.

To make the holiness of God even more awesome, the transcendent God has come close to us. It would be one thing to know that God was gloriously transcendent and entirely separate from his creation. In such a situation we could become accustomed to his lack of intervention in human affairs, and for practical purposes we could become our own gods. But our God is also the Immanent One who has revealed himself and become like us. He said, "I will be your God and you will be my people" (Lev. 26:12). He is near us. He will never leave us or forsake us (Heb. 13:5). He is so close he calls us "friends" (John 15:14). He is so close, the Scripture talks about Christ *in* you (Col. 1:27). Given his nature, this is virtually impossible for us to grasp. But, by God's grace, we can grow in knowing his holiness, and this knowledge will both expel the people-idols from our lives and leave us less prone to being consumed with ourselves.

What Opposes the Fear of the Lord?

The problem we encounter in our quest to know and fear the Lord as he ought to be feared is that we have three prominent adversaries. The world, our own flesh, and the Devil conspire to elevate other people (or what we can get from them) over God.

The resistance is actually found in our heart (flesh), and it is influenced by the world and the Devil. Our hearts have dozens of strategies to avoid the fear of the Lord. One strategy is that we downgrade obedience—the concrete expression of the fear of the Lord—into concern about appearances. We concentrate on actions and overlook attitudes. By doing this, our sinful nature can give us a sense that we are okay. We have not killed today. We have not been adulterous. We have not stolen anything from the store. Therefore, we had a good day. Better yet, we *are* good. Of course, we occasionally do bad things. We might yell too loudly, or we might pick up some pornography at the airport. In these cases we should ask God's forgiveness. But, on the whole, we tend to be fairly good. And if we think we are usually good, then God is usually irrelevant.

Such thinking is not advertised as good theology, but isn't it the practical theology of most Christians? I know that it can be my own. I am a good guy—a nice guy—who occasionally does bad things. Such thinking ignores the depths of sin in my own heart, and, in essence, it elevates me so that I am just a mildly flawed imitation of God rather than someone completely dependent on him. Fear of the Lord is then impossible.

To make sin even more difficult to see, it often rides on the back of many good things. For example, work is a good thing, but sin can take it and exalt it to the point where it rules us. We become workaholics who say we are doing it for the kids, but we are really doing it for ourselves. What about financial planning? Isn't it wise to establish a nest egg for the future? This, too, is a good thing, but it can grow to ruling proportions and we forsake generosity. Most sins are ungodly exaggerations of things that are good. As a result, we can supply proof texts to justify our behavior long after it has become idolatrous.

The world takes these tendencies and rationalizes them. The world reminds us that, whatever our sins or "shortcomings," we are only human. Everyone else is doing it too. Right and wrong are determined by popular vote. And who is to say that God really cares about such things? The world suggests that God is real but far away. He got everything started but now he is sitting back, letting things happen. The world says that we live in a deistic universe where there may be a god, but "God helps those who help themselves."

The Devil stands against anything that can exalt the true God. Whenever we fear anything—a god, a person, or anything in the subhuman creation—other than God, Satan is basking in the darkness we have created. By lies and other deceptions, he minimizes our sin, he suggests that God is distant and that God's Word cannot really be trusted. In fact, he suggests that God is holding out on us, keeping us from good things.

With such adversaries, growing in the fear of the Lord will not be a smooth process. Instead, it will be the path of warfare. We must hate the evil and ungodly assumptions of the world, we must hate our own sinful nature, and we must hate Satan. To accomplish these tasks demands the most powerful resources we have: the Word, the Spirit, and the body of Christ.

Learning the Fear of the Lord

Adversaries should not discourage us, however. The fear of the Lord can certainly be learned. Deuteronomy 4:10 states, "Assemble the people before me [the Lord] to hear my words so that they may learn to revere [fear] me as long as they live in the land." Likewise, King David exhorted the people to learn the fear of the Lord.

> *Fear the LORD, you his saints, for those who fear him lack nothing. . . . Come, my children, listen to me; I will teach you the fear of the LORD. (Ps. 34:9, 11)*

How is it learned? By reading and meditating on the Word, and by praying that our God would teach us.

> *When he [the king] takes the throne of his kingdom, he is to write for himself on a scroll a copy of this law, taken from that of the priests, who are Levites. It is to be with him, and he is to read it all the days of his life so that he may learn to revere the LORD his God and follow carefully all the words of this law." (Deut. 17:18–19)*

> *Their children, who do not know this law, must hear it and learn to fear the LORD your God. (Deut. 31:13)*

This is not easy. Consistent Bible reading can be tough. The three adversaries make sure it is a battle, and our worlds are already too busy. But if the fear of the Lord is as important as Scripture indicates, then we can be sure that God himself will give us the power to pursue it.

Consider how you can use the resources that God has given you. Ask your spouse, children, friends, pastor, or elders to pray for you. Meet with a brother or sister. Ask them how they have witnessed the awesome God. Start identifying where the world tries to remake God so that he is more manageable. Ask God to teach you to read his Word as a wise person who "looks *intently* into the perfect law that gives freedom" (James 1:25).

Now consider a few of the passages that teach the fear of the Lord. Since the entire Bible teaches that the Holy One of Israel reigns, the entire Bible is a textbook on the fear of the Lord, whether it uses that particular expression or not. But there are some passages that seem to be especially pivotal—or neglected. I'll focus on some of these.

Notice especially the mighty acts of God that show both his holy love *and* justice, kindness *and* sternness (Rom. 11:22). The psalmist reminds us that those who fear the Lord say, "His love endures forever" (Ps. 118:4), but they also say, "Who can stand before you when you are angry?" (Ps. 76:7). Scripture speaks of unimaginable love alongside holy anger. God is compassionate and gracious, slow to anger and abounding in love, but he also does not leave the guilty unpunished; "he punishes the children and their children for the sin of the fathers to the third and fourth generation" (Ex. 34:6,7). Therefore, we cannot rightly say, "My God is not a God of judgment and anger; my God is a God of love." Such thinking makes it almost impossible to grow in the fear of the Lord. It suggests that sin only saddens God rather than offends him. Both justice and love are expressions of his holiness, and we must know both to learn the fear of the Lord. If we look only at God's love, we will not need him, and there will be no urgency in the message of the cross. If we focus narrowly on God's justice, we will want to avoid him, and we will live in terror-fear, always feeling guilty and waiting for punishment.

Learning the Fear of the Lord the Creator

Consider the Bible God's school in the fear of the Lord. Class begins immediately. The Bible opens by teaching that the Holy One reigns.

> *Let all the earth fear the LORD;*
> *let all the people of the world revere him.*

Chapter Six

For he spoke, and it came to be;
he commanded, and it stood firm. (Ps. 33:8–9)

Creation is God's servant. He spoke just one word and it existed to do his will. What we see around us is God's handiwork that even *he* said was good. If God said it was good, it must be quite a work of art, even in its presently marred form.

More specifically, I can consider that traditional majestic landmark, the Grand Canyon, a truly remarkable piece of desert. The memory of it certainly points me to the bigness of God. But I should be careful. God is holy. He is above anything we could think or see. The Grand Canyon points to someone incomprehensibly grander (Ps. 93:3–4).

Even more than the Grand Canyon, I prefer considering the ocean. I worked as a lifeguard on the beach for five summers and never grew tired of its expanse. I have been cooled by it as a reminder of God's refreshing grace, and I have been battered by it as a reminder of God's great power. God's ocean reminds me that he is much bigger than any person.

Look around and notice God's glory reflected in creation. The blue of the sky reflects his royal garment. The clouds are reminders of his presence (Ex. 19:9), they are his chariot as he oversees his creation (Ps. 104:3). The winds are his messengers (Ps. 104:4). They come from the storehouses of God (Ps. 135:7). The sun comes forth like a bridegroom, reminding me that Jesus is returning for his church (Ps. 19:5). The heavens truly praise his wonders (Ps. 89:5), they declare his glory (Ps. 19:1).

Every animal you see drinking or feeding on the grass is being sustained by the Most High God (Ps. 104). The farmer did not cause the crops to grow. The crops come from the ground as a gift from God. Rain is an expression of his care, lightning of his power.

Furthermore, God owns creation. "In his hand are the depths of the earth, and the mountain peaks belong to him" (Ps. 95:4). We are walking on privately owned land.

Elizabeth Barrett Browning put it this way:

> *Earth's crammed with heaven,*
> *And every bush afire with God;*
> *But only he who sees takes off his shoes;*
> *The rest sit around it and pluck blackberries.*[2]

The psalmist preceded Elizabeth Barrett Browning in taking off his shoes. The majesty of creation inspired his worship and humility.

> *When I consider your heavens,*
> *the work of your fingers,*
> *the moon and the stars,*
> *which you have set in place,*
> *what is man that you are mindful of him,*
> *the son of man that you care for him? (Ps. 8:3–4)*

With all the created beauty around us, beauty that certainly exceeds our own in many ways, God chose people to be the crown of his creation.

Like the psalmist, I have two basic responses to this truth. Neither of them really pumps up my self-esteem. First, I am simply amazed. I am filled with questions: Why, O Lord, did you ever bother with us? Why, with all this beauty in your creation, did you make people your distinct image-bearers? Certainly I am grateful, but it is hard to believe that God would place us over his creation.

---

2 Elizabeth Barrett Browning, "Aurora Leigh," Book VII.

Chapter Six

My second response is that I am humbled. Both the Grand Canyon and the oceans are a good bit more beautiful than I am. This, instead of bolstering self-esteem, ruins it. I am not living beautifully. My heart is too often compromised with concerns about *my* glory rather than God's. The hurt from this humbling, however, is exactly what I need. It feels a lot better than any temporary puffing up of my ego.

Jacob and Moses Learn the Fear of the Lord

When reading Genesis through the lens of the fear of the Lord, every event becomes more dramatic. The flood is an awesome display of God's justice; Noah is an awesome evidence of his love. The Tower of Babel demonstrates God's great power and justice; he will not let man glorify himself. But Babel also demonstrates God's great love in that he limits the effects of a leader's sin. With people scattered throughout the world and living in distinct clans, there is less opportunity for one person to oppress many. The call of Abraham is a fearful (that is, beautiful, awesome) picture of love that pursues. The transcendent God comes close to a man and calls him to be the father of many people—God's people. Each story challenges our limited understanding of God's justice and love, and each can lead us to reverence the Lord. But only the story of Jacob reveals God by the name "Fear" (Gen. 31:53).

The first time Jacob met God, or the Fear of Isaac, as he called him, he was on the run from his brother Esau. Having just cheated him out of the birthright, Jacob had reason to fear the man. Esau was bigger, stronger, and perhaps more volatile. Undoubtedly, at this time in Jacob's life, man was big and God was small.

Jacob's dream (Gen. 28:10–22) changed all that. The word "holy" is used throughout the Bible, but it is most often used as a description of the dwelling place of God. This is where Jacob found himself.

In a dream, the curtain of heaven parted and the Lord spoke. The words, indeed, were tender and comforting, but they were still holy. Therefore, Jacob was afraid; he was glad to awake alive. He exclaimed, "How awesome is this place," and he vowed that "the LORD will be my God" (Gen. 28:21). He called the place Bethel, meaning house of God.

It was this event that was most likely in Jacob's mind when he called God "the Fear of Isaac." It was not, however, Jacob's only encounter with God. The context of the next meeting with God was similar in that it included the threat of Esau, but it is different in that Jacob was going to meet Esau rather than run from him.

The question was clear: Whom will you fear? Esau or the true God? To help Jacob with this decision, God blessed him with a visitation even more intimate than the dream at Bethel. God actually appeared to Jacob as a man, wrestled with him, and then blessed him.

Can you imagine? It is one thing for God to reveal himself in a dream; it is something completely different for God to literally get dirty with his people. Yet this is the way God delights in revealing himself to us. He is the one who is close, he is God-with-us. Such exposure to the character of God was too much for Jacob, so God chose to keep his name a mystery. With us, however, the mystery has been revealed. We know the wrestler by the name that inspires *the* most reverence and awe—"at the name of Jesus every knee should bow" (Phil. 2:10).

Can you already get a sense of the expulsive power of the fear of the Lord? A growing knowledge of God displaces the fear of people, and it casts out our tendency to be casual with our secret sins. And the good news is that it can be learned. God is absolutely enthusiastic about blessing us with this knowledge. You don't have to be a patriarch of Israel. You simply must be a person who prays (Eph.

1:17) and seeks after this great gift. You can also learn from others who have learned the fear of the Lord.

Moses, like Jacob, was not a natural God-fearer, but he certainly learned the fear of the Lord. His first Bethel experience occurred while he too was on the run. He was in the wilderness, hiding from Pharaoh, when God appeared to him as a fire. In other words, God brought his dwelling near to Moses and declared it holy ground. Moses was commanded to take off his sandals, and he hid his face because he was afraid.

Both Jacob and Moses received blessings and promises—a knowledge of God's love is essential to reverential fear—but both men were afraid of the closeness of the Most High God. To place them on the fear continuum from dread to worship, they go from one extreme to the other. Their fear of the Lord was characterized by terror as well as worship. In this they are good examples. In the life of the Christian, the momentum moves from the dread related to judgment to the worship motivated by love. However, these biblical examples suggest that trembling is also suited to the believer. It is good for us to have times when we are uncomfortable before God. It may not be a fear of punishment, but it may be a fear of incurring God's displeasure. Or it may simply be the fear (reverence) that is unavoidable when seeing God in his glory. When we are sensitive to the demands of his holiness, we can be led by Moses, Jacob, and the psalmist to say, "My flesh trembles in fear of you" (Ps. 119:120). One of God's names is "Fear."

The Lessons of the Exodus

We learn the fear of the Lord by knowing God the Creator. The universe is certainly an expression of his power and love. We also learn the fear of the Lord by witnessing God as redeemer. In the Old Testament, this is seen most clearly in the exodus from Egypt.

The exodus from Egypt and the law that was given from Sinai were some of the first large scale classes in the fear of the Lord. During these events, God demonstrated that he alone was God. Nothing could compare to him. In power and judgment, and in love and faithfulness, God had no equal.

After the Israelites left Egypt, they were eventually led to the mountain of God. Being close to God's abode, they were commanded to symbolically cleanse themselves and be separated: they could not touch the foot of the mountain, they washed their clothes, and they abstained from sexual relations when they convened around the mountain. They had to prepare themselves to be close to holy ground.

What they witnessed was astounding. Fire descended on the mountain; smoke was everywhere. The entire mountain trembled, and the sound of the trumpet, announcing the coming of God, grew louder and louder. The senses of the people must have been pushed to the limit.

I once experienced something almost as loud and overwhelming. I had been driving for about twenty hours with some college friends en route to southern Florida. By the time we arrived it was around one-thirty in morning. The motels seemed too expensive for such a short night, so we decided to find a place to put up a tent. Meanwhile, we were all, except for the driver, falling in and out of sleep. When he finally stopped, we set up the tent, and slept for the night. What we didn't know was that in his haste to find a temporary campsite, the driver went past a "No Trespassing" sign.

The next thing I remember was the earth shaking and the sound of mountains falling. In the commotion, all I noticed was that the mouths of my four friends were wide open, and the veins of their necks were popping out. They were screaming, but the noise outside was so deafening that I couldn't hear anything from them. After a few moments of imitating the Keystone Kops, we finally stumbled out of the tent and learned why we had a free campsite. We had camped right beside the end of a military runway. The noise we'd heard was a huge military transport plane that took off within thirty feet of our heads.

I suspect that the Israelites couldn't hear the shrieks from their neighbors either when the trumpets sounded. But they were most likely too preoccupied with the mountain to notice open mouths and veins popping out.

The result was ten words on two tablets of stone—the law. Does that seem anticlimactic? With such fanfare the people might have expected more than two stone tablets. At least there could have been two tablets of gold. Yet if they were expecting something more magnificent, they completely missed the nature of the law.

The law is wonderful in that it reveals the holy character of God. The Ten Commandments and their many applications teach about the Lawgiver. They reveal that God's ways are profoundly higher than the ways of the surrounding nations. What may seem like nit-picking to us was actually a beautiful revelation of the God who protected the oppressed and poor, hated injustice, loved mercy, offered forgiveness and cleansing, and was morally pure. In the law, God set a new standard for holiness that the world had not known.

We could also say that the law is a document of holy love. In it God says, "I have just shown you that, even though you were one of the weakest of nations, I rescued you and cared for you as my beloved child. I have revealed more of my everlasting love for you. Now that you have seen my love and know that you are my children, you must learn how to love me and live like divine children. To show you how to do this, I give you the law. It will teach you how to be like your heavenly Father."

I am the LORD your God; consecrate yourselves and be holy, because I am holy. (Lev. 11:44)

Speak to the entire assembly of Israel and say to them: "Be holy because I, the LORD your God, am holy." (Lev. 19:2)

Consecrate yourselves and be holy, because I am the LORD your God. (Lev. 20:7)

You are to be holy to me because I, the LORD, am holy, and I have set you apart from the nations to be my own. (Lev. 20:26)

How will the people become holy? How will they love and glorify their God? In reverence they will submit to God's authority and obey him. This is what the fear of the Lord looks like. This is what the law can teach. What more majestic gift could there be? No wonder the psalmist said, "My flesh trembles in fear of you; I stand in awe of your laws" (Ps. 119:120).

This is the third class in the fear of the Lord. At this point, make sure that you keep your eyes on the Holy One. Whether the subject is the Grand Canyon or the Ten Commandments, these inspire awe because they are an expression of the holy character of God.

GROW IN THE FEAR
OF THE LORD

THE problem is clear: People are too big in our lives and God is too small. The answer is straightforward: We must learn to know that our God is more loving and more powerful than we ever imagined. Yet this task is not easy. Even if we worked at the most spectacular of national parks, or the bush in our backyard started burning without being consumed, or Jesus appeared and wrestled a few rounds with us, we would not be guaranteed a persistent reverence of God. Too often our mountain-top experiences are quickly overtaken by the clamor of the world, and God once again is diminished in our minds. The goal is to establish a *daily* tradition of growing in the knowledge of God.

The Fear of the Lord: Its Beauty

To grow in the knowledge of the Holy God we must find such knowledge beautiful and attractive. This is where the book of Proverbs can help. The heart of the book is the fear of the Lord: it is the gateway, the path, and the end of wisdom—"The fear of the

LORD is the beginning of wisdom, and knowledge of the Holy One is understanding" (Prov. 9:10).

Since the fear of the Lord is the great treasure of life, Proverbs tries to woo us to it. It tries to make the fear of the Lord as attractive as possible. Those who fear the Lord will fear nothing else (19:23). The fear of the Lord adds length to life (10:27), it is a secure fortress for the one who fears *and* for his or her children (14:26). It is a fountain of life (15:16), it brings honor (22:4), and it should be praised when we see it (31:30).

What does the fear of the Lord look like? It looks like loving good and hating evil. "The fear of the LORD is to hate evil" (8:13). It looks like trusting God (reverence) and obeying him.

Can you see that the fear of the Lord is a blessing? Just imagine what it would be like to truly hate sin, first our own, then the sins of others (Matt. 7:3–5). What would happen to marital fights? They would be almost impossible. Spouses would be too busy listening and asking forgiveness for their own selfishness. What about the little cliques in the school yard? They would be telling *good* stories about somebody else. What about when someone sins against us? We would no longer have to murder the person in our own heart. Instead, we could cover the sin in humility and love, or we could confront the other person in the same spirit.

As you read through the following stories, keep in mind some examples from your own life where people have been bigger than God. And remember that these people who control you are harmless kittens when compared to the Lion of Judah.

The Fear of the Lord: God's Questions

"Have you considered my servant Job?" the Lord asked Satan. Job is a near-perfect example of a person who feared the Lord. If you want to know whether or not you fear God, note your reaction when good things are taken from you. How do you react to financial loss, the death of a family member, the loss of love? How many of us, after experiencing such intense suffering, would be persuaded that God is bigger than our suffering? Job certainly was. After losing everything, he said, "The LORD gave and the LORD has taken away; may the name of the LORD be praised" (Job 1:21). Then, after his own body was severely afflicted, he said, "Shall we accept good from God, and not trouble?" (Job 2:10). Job is the first to talk specifically about *wisdom* and the fear of the Lord when he said, "The fear of the Lord—that is wisdom, and to shun evil is understanding" (Job 28:28). But even with these statements, it is not Job's words that are the most instructive.

Apart from the giving of the law, God's longest speech in the entire Bible is in the last four chapters of Job. It is a speech intended to cause Job to grow even more in knowing God's greatness. If you read these chapters every day for a month you will find that they are a treatment for almost anything. Do you fear people? Are you suffering? Are you anxious? Depressed? Struggling with anger? Hard-hearted? Listen to these questions from the mouth of God.

"Have you ever given orders to the morning?" (38:12)

"Have you seen the gates of the shadow of death? Have you comprehended the vast expanses of the earth?" (38:17–18)

"Do you send the lightning bolts on their way? Do they report to you, 'Here we are'?" (38:35)

The pace of God's questions is relentless. They leave you speechless. But they are graciously delivered to a righteous man who prizes the fear of the Lord above all else. The effect of God's words was exactly what was intended: Job's response demonstrated that he understood that God was holy—God was above him. God's knowledge was "too wonderful for me to know." God was different than Job. He was not like a man who could be summoned. As further evidence of Job's growth in the fear of the Lord, he humbled himself before the Almighty. "I despise myself and repent in dust and ashes" (Job 42: 6). Such humility and repentance are a sure sign that we are learning the fear of the Lord.

Can you remember times in your life when you said, "God is God—I submit to his will"? At those times other people have no power to manipulate, pressure, or control us.

The Fear of the Lord: Face to Face

While Job's class in the fear of the Lord was not specifically targeted to the fear of other people, God's instruction to the prophet Isaiah certainly was. When Isaiah was called by God, he was given a message that guaranteed he would be rejected and physically threatened by others (Isa. 6:9–14). There were going to be daily opportunities for him to fear man rather than God. As a result, it was essential for him to have the fear of the Lord absolutely branded into his heart, because the person who fears God fears nothing else.

Think of it. God tells you to speak out publicly against national policy in such a way that you will be declared a traitor. You are invited to a banquet and have to preach doom and gloom to the revelers. You will be *the* most unpopular person in all of Israel and Judah, and kings will want your head. In such situations God gives his people special grace. For Isaiah, this grace came as a kind of ordination sermon. The impact of this ordination gave shape to the entire book, and it is the reason Isaiah prefers to call his God the Holy One of Israel.

"In the year that King Uzziah died" (Isa. 6:1), begins Isaiah. With this introduction, Isaiah is not trying to give us a historical marker for the events that follow; he is introducing the fear of the Lord.

King Uzziah was a marvelous king. Schooled by Zechariah in the fear of God (2 Chron. 26:5), the Lord gave him success after success. However, he did not heed the law's instruction to be especially alert during the days of prosperity. When he became powerful, in his pride he usurped a task specifically delegated to the priests alone. The result was that the Lord afflicted him immediately with leprosy.

It brings back memories of Moses. Here was a truly fine leader who tripped at just one point and was severely disciplined. Moses was not allowed to enter the promised land, and Uzziah was struck with leprosy until the day he died. Therefore, when Uzziah died, it was a time of national mourning, and it was also a time to grow in the fear of the Lord. The Lord was a holy God who would not tolerate sin in his people. So Isaiah was trembling even before the vision.

Isaiah was in the temple, most likely thinking about Uzziah, when God opened his eyes to heavenly realities.

> *I saw the Lord seated on a throne, high and exalted, and the train of his robe filled the temple. Above him were seraphs, each with six wings: With two wings they covered their faces, with two they covered their feet, and with two they were flying. (Isa. 6:1–2)*

Isaiah saw the Lord, seated on the throne, wearing priestly robes. His holy presence dominated the temple. It was so dominating that the seraphs had to hover *above* the throne. There was no room around it.

These seraphs are mentioned only in Isaiah and nowhere else in the Bible. The fact that Isaiah was unfamiliar with them made the scene even more stunning. A more recognizable, familiar angel might have made the scene a little easier on him. "If they can stand before God, maybe I can too." But Isaiah was completely unprepared for these creatures. He had never even heard of them. The closest thing to these creatures were the cherubim that were on top of the ark of the covenant, but even these were found only in the Holy of Holies.

The seraphs appeared to have only one job—calling out about the holiness of the Lord. They were so majestic that *their* voices shook the threshold of the temple. But even with such an elevated status, the seraphs still needed to be covered from the holy gaze of God.

They called out to each other: "Holy, holy, holy is the LORD Almighty; the whole earth is full of his glory." The thrice-holy magnifies the holiness of God. Each "holy" intensifies the one before it.

My daughter taught me about the power of such repetition. One afternoon I was working in my study at home. When I'm there, I prefer not to be interrupted. It is an unwritten and unspoken guideline, but I have probably been grumpy when interrupted in the past, so my daughters usually leave me alone. But this particular afternoon, Lisa really wanted to play with me. She asked me when I would be done, and then hung around, looking over my shoulder, hoping it would be soon. Such temptation was too much for me, so I took the afternoon off and played with her. It meant I had to work that evening, but it was worth it.

Before she went to bed she slipped a note into my hand.

Dear Daddy,
I love you so, so, so, so, so, so . . . so much.
Love Lisa
xxxxxxxxxxxxxxoooooooooooooo

For two pages she repeated "so."

She didn't have the vocabulary to say "exceedingly" or the poetic ability to use a rich metaphor. If she had, the letter would have been less powerful. Instead, every "so" intensified the "so" before it. She was saying that it was impossible for her to love me more than she did.

This is how I learned to take notice of "Holy, holy, holy."

Isaiah did what anybody would do. He cried out, "Woe to me!" He was certain that he would die. He was unclean, and he was in the presence of the Holy One of Israel who had punished Uzziah with leprosy.

Yet the Lord was not done with Isaiah. This was a school in the fear of the Lord, and the pinnacle of the teaching consists of the mingling of power and judgment with gentleness and loving forgiveness. Therefore, in an act that points to Jesus as clearly as anything in the Bible, the seraph took the initiative toward a man who was as good as dead. The seraph purified Isaiah by taking hot coals from the altar where sacrifices were offered to God, and touching him (1 John 1:9).

Then Isaiah did what anybody would do in such a situation. He forgot about himself and offered himself as a servant to the living God. His fear of the Lord was expressed by reverential obedience. This is one of the great blessings of the fear of the Lord. We think less often about ourselves. When a heart is being filled with the greatness of God, there is less room for the question, "What are people going to think of me?"

If you have ever walked among giant redwoods, you will never be overwhelmed by the size of a dogwood tree. Or if you have been through a hurricane, a spring rain is nothing to fear. If you have been in the presence of the almighty God, everything that once controlled you suddenly has less power.

I remember being in a small group with a man who was frightened to say anything that might upset anyone. As a result, he was quiet and hesitant with his wife, he rarely disciplined his children, and his boss terrified him. We realized that this man's father had been unpredictable with his own anger, but our insights into this past relationship did not liberate this man. Finally, after weeks of trying to help, the group focused on something else. We looked at the pictures of God in the book of Isaiah. After four meetings, this frightened man asked for prayer—he was going to speak with his boss about some practices in the office that he believed were unfair. The knowledge of God was the first step in his liberation from the fear of people.

The pictures of God included the throne scene in Isaiah 6, yet there are many more. Throughout the book we see pictures of God's holy justice and God's great compassion for his people. By the time we get to Isaiah 40, these two themes play tag with each other until they are finally wedded in Isaiah 53.

"Comfort, comfort my people, says your God." Isaiah 40 begins a section of prophecies that culminate in the message of the cross. The Lord didn't say, "Comfort." He said, "Comfort, comfort." He underlined the motherly care that he gives to those in exile. The greatest comfort God could give was to be present with his people. The reason they are in exile was because they left the presence of the Holy One. Now the Holy One was returning to claim his people. He was coming close.

Among the voices that announced his coming was one that called out, "All men are like grass, and all their glory is like the flowers of the field" (40:6). Although this voice sounds quite disheartening, it offered words of comfort. The comfort was that the king of Assyria—the oppressor of God's people—would pass away like the withering flowers. Even though the people would go into exile because of their own sin, it would not last forever, because the king of Assyria was merely a man and not God. His power could not overturn God's eternal promises to his people.

God was coming to rescue his people from threats, attacks, and captivity. With the same mighty arm that saved the people over and over, and the same mighty arm that judged Israel, he would now hold young lambs close to his heart.

> *He tends his flock like a shepherd:*
> *He gathers the lambs in his arms*
> *and carries them close to his heart;*
> *he gently leads those that have young. (Isa. 40:11)*

When we are being oppressed by other people—whether they are enemies, bosses, or spouses—this is one of the holy pictures that God gives us. "Oppression will not last," God says, "but my compassion will." God's compassion is bigger than the threats of other people. This, of course, is difficult to see at times. It takes eyes of faith to see God's strong arms of compassion and anticipate deliverance in times of trouble. But God's goodness to us is always close, and we need to practice seeing it.

Following this precious picture of God's shepherd-like care of his people, God then goes into a Job-like series of questions. How does this fit with the pictures of his immense compassion? They both lead us into the fear of the Lord. The God who is over all things, and the God who comes close to his people in mercy and forgiveness is to be feared.

> *Who has measured the waters in the hollow of his hand,*
> *or with the breadth of his hand marked off the heavens?...*
> *Before him all the nations are as nothing;*

they are regarded as worthless
and less than nothing. (vv. 12, 17)

The refrain, repeated twice in this prophecy, summarizes the fear of the Lord.

To whom, then, will you compare God?
What image will you compare him to? (v. 18)

Although these words seem to be lifted out of the text of Job, there is a very significant difference between the two. With Job, the Lord was speaking privately. This time, the Lord was speaking to the entire world. He was even addressing the distant islands (Isa. 41:1). God never intended to be the tribal God of Israel alone. His glory is too great to be confined to any particular group. His glory is such that it demands the attention of all mankind (Isa. 40:5). He is, indeed, a big God.

The story of this worldwide glory builds to a climax in Isaiah 52 and 53. Yet, at first glance, it is not the end we hope for. Instead, this story ends with an ugly, suffering servant. Isaiah 52 starts fittingly enough. People are bursting into joy, captives are being freed, the mountains around Jerusalem are beautiful, and all the earth will witness the salvation of the Lord. All this celebration is a result of the servant of the Lord who will restore the tribes of Israel.

See, my servant will act wisely;
he will be raised and lifted up and highly exalted. (v. 13)

But it abruptly turns into something almost macabre.

Just as there were many who were appalled at him—

his appearance was so disfigured beyond that of any man
and his form marred beyond human likeness—
so he will sprinkle many nations,
and kings will shut their mouths because of him. (vv.
14–15)

Glory will be realized through suffering and death. Not our own suffering and death, because the text clearly points to a servant who will represent us. Exaltation will come through God's "crushing" the servant. And all this will be done for us.

For he bore the sins of many,
and made intercession for the transgressors. (53:12)

This is the Old Testament zenith of the holiness of God. If your jaw doesn't drop when you read it, then read it again. Read and be in awe.

Such awe attracts you to God; it does not repel or leave you feeling shame. It makes you want to come to him and know him. When the fear of the Lord matures in you, Christ becomes irresistible.

Do you find yourself on the "hiding from God" end of the continuum? Or do you still find yourself not on the continuum at all? If so, Jesus says, "Come … come … come" (Isa. 55:1). He invites you to come close. He invites you to know him as the Glorious One he is. If that invitation doesn't stir you, remember that he does not say, "Come," just once; he repeats it to you. He could not have expressed his invitation more lovingly.

The Fear of the Lord: God's Wrath

Jesus, the servant of whom Isaiah spoke, was crushed for us; therefore, if we believe and turn from our sins, we are not crushed.

We have been rescued from deadly peril and endless pain. But as we get farther from the day we were rescued, do we remember what we were saved from? Do we remember that we should have been crushed by God's wrath? Do we realize that, from our perspective, the cross is the greatest injustice that there will ever be? The Perfect One crushed in place of sinners? And do we remember that there will be a divine judgment when God's wrath will be revealed (Rom. 2:5)? Hell teaches us about the fear of the Lord.

Today, the majority of Americans believe in God, heaven, and angels, but fewer and fewer believe there is a hell. Hell is unpopular even among conservative Bible students. I suspect, however, that it is not so much that hell is unpopular these days. Perhaps it is *too* popular.

Let me explain. We know God, we have a conscience that tells us right from wrong. We know that we do not measure up to God's glory, and we know we deserve his wrath. But the thought of hell is too terrible to face. Remember, we prefer to think about low self-image rather than nakedness before God. We are good at avoiding the holiness of God. In the same way, there are powerful spiritual forces that lead us to minimize the terror of hell.

Jesus, the one who rescues us from hell, is also the one who speaks the most about it. He is the "scare" preacher, the divine threatener. Here are some examples of his words:

Anyone who says, "You fool!" will be in danger of the fire of hell. (Matt. 5:22)

Every tree that does not bear good fruit is cut down and thrown into the fire. (Matt. 7:19)

If your hand causes you to sin, cut it off. It is better for you to enter life maimed than with two hands to go into hell, where the fire never goes out. (Mark 9:43–44)

Whoever believes in him [Jesus] is not condemned, but whoever does not believe stands condemned already. (John 3:18)

Then he will say to those on his left, "Depart from me, you who are cursed, into the eternal fire prepared for the devil and his angels." (Matt. 25:41)

Consider Matthew 10:28, "Do not be afraid of those who kill the body but cannot kill the soul. Rather, be afraid of the One who can destroy both soul and body in hell." John Calvin said that this text makes one's hair stand on end.

Jonathan Edwards was a preacher who tried to imitate Jesus. As a result, he preached a number of sermons on hell. His most famous sermon on hell left people trembling right into a revival called the Great Awakening. Jonathan Edwards had first delivered it to his Northampton, Massachusetts church, but we have no record of the response. It was at a meetinghouse in Enfield, Connecticut, on July 8, 1741, where we are familiar with the impact of "Sinners in the Hands of an Angry God." This sermon was certainly not the most frightening of his sermons; "The Justice of God in the Damnation of Sinners" and Edwards's sermon on Romans 2:4 were more severe. But God used "Sinners in the Hands of an Angry God" to incite the fear of the Lord. These excerpts illustrate why:

> There is nothing that keeps wicked men at any one moment out of hell, but the mere pleasure of God. ... The wrath of God is like great waters that are dammed for the present; they increase more and more, and rise higher and higher, till an outlet is given; and

the longer the stream is stopped, the more rapid and mighty is its course, when once it is let loose.

The God that holds you over the pit of hell, much as one holds a spider, or loathsome insect, over the flame. . . . His wrath towards you burns like fire . . . he is of purer eyes than to bear to have you in His sight. . . . You have offended him infinitely more than ever a stubborn rebel did his prince. . . .

O sinner! Consider the fearful danger you are in: It is a great furnace of wrath, a wide and bottomless pit. . . . You hang by a slender thread, with the flames of divine wrath flashing about it.[1]

His listeners had a biblically appropriate response. They literally cried out so loud that they made it difficult for Edwards to continue. They were actually falling off their pews into the aisles because they were overwhelmed with the holiness of God. It may not have been a mature fear of the Lord, but it was a good place to start.

Here is the truth about hell. When a person dies apart from faith in Jesus, there is no possible deliverance from eternal hell (Matt. 25:46). There is no relief from torment (Rom. 2:4), and, worst of all, it is the holy wrath of God that is poured out (John 3:36). Such knowledge led the apostle Paul to say, "Since, then, we know what it is to fear the Lord, we try to persuade men" (2 Cor. 5:11).[2]

This is what we deserve; this is the wrath and "crushing" that Jesus took on himself for us. We should tremble at the thought. We should tremble because it could have been us who were crushed because of our sin. We should tremble because we live in the presence of a divine love that is absolutely astonishing. And, against

1   *The Works of Jonathan Edwards* (New York: Leavitt and Allen, 1855), 4:313–21.
2   A helpful book is Robert A. Peterson, *Hell on Trial: The Case for Eternal Punishment* (Phillipsburg, N.J.: Presbyterian and Reformed, 1995).

the backdrop of hell, we should tremble at the thought of heaven. How could it possibly be? We who were naked before God, who deserved eternal wrath, are by faith blessed by the Father. It is one thing to release a person from prison, but it is something else to deluge that same person with all the riches imaginable. But that is what our God has done. We are given an inheritance, "the kingdom prepared for you since the creation of the world" (Matt. 25:34). How could this be?

O Lord, what is man that you are mindful of him? We respond to your mercy and love, not with a slavish fear and worldly sorrow, but with a reverence that leads us to repentance and a delight to trust you and obey.

The Fear of the Lord: Amazement

There are many other biblical themes and passages that direct us to the fear of the Lord. The gospel of Mark, however, is the book of amazement. It is constantly saying that Jesus amazed those who witnessed his ministry. This amazement did not always lead to reverent submission, but it is Mark's way of teaching us that Jesus is the Holy One, God in the flesh.

Mark's basic theme is that Jesus amazed people by both his teaching and his miraculous deeds. He starts this theme immediately: "The people were amazed at his teaching" (Mark 1:22). Mark's gospel proceeds to show Jesus' demonstrating authority over evil spirits (1:27). Then, when Jesus told the paralytic that his sins were forgiven and he could walk, everyone was amazed and praised God (2:12).

The next story of amazement took the disciples back to the creation account and the creative word of God. Crowds were already following Jesus to the point where a boat was one of the few places where he could rest. "Let us go over to the other side," Jesus said to his disciples. After they rowed beyond view of the shore, a furious storm came up, threatening to capsize the boat. Waves were already breaking over the sides and the boat was filling up with water. How Jesus could ever sleep through such an event seems superhuman in itself, but that is not what caused the amazement. When the disciples could finally shake him awake, Jesus spoke to his creation. "Quiet! Be still!" And the water became flat as glass.

Prior to this time, the disciples had seen and heard many things. They had witnessed many miraculous healings, and they had heard teaching that elicited as much awe from the crowds as did the miracles. But this is the first time that Mark talks about the disciples' responses.

How would you respond if you were standing next to the Creator God and heard him speak to his creation? Don't forget, even the words of the seraphim could shake the temple.

"They were terrified," Mark says about the disciples. They did not feel relief or happiness that they would live and not even lose their boat. They were terrified.

What a wonderful response. It was ideal for people being schooled in the fear of the Lord.

This was only the beginning. Mark wants us to know that the entire ministry of Jesus was punctuated with amazement. The people were amazed when he cast evil spirits into the pigs (5:20). When Jairus' daughter was raised from the dead, her parents were completely astonished (5:42). When Jesus taught in the synagogue, many who heard were amazed (6:2). When the Pharisees tried to trap him and Jesus turned the occasion into a display of wisdom, the witnesses were amazed (12:17). When he walked on water the disciples were amazed (6:51). When he healed a deaf and mute man, people were overwhelmed and amazed (7:37). The crowds were even "overwhelmed and filled with wonder" at the very sight of Jesus (9:15). Yet among these events, there is no clear evidence that amazement turned quickly toward faith, except with one particular woman (5:25–34).

There are a number of mysteries in this latter event. How did Jesus know that "power had gone out from him" (5:30), and how could the woman have thought that touching Jesus alone would have healed her? Jesus' healings were usually accompanied by a word or a specific act. What made her think that a clandestine touch would heal?

"If I just touch his clothes, I will be healed" (Mark 5:28), she thought. It was her faith that singled her out. Jesus was touched by thousands of people, but, up to this point, there was only one person singled out as having faith. She had spent everything she had on medical treatments and her bleeding only became worse. Yet when she heard Jesus was coming, she believed he could heal her. This, indeed, is great faith. After dozens of treatments this woman had certainly given up hope. Sure, she might try the next treatment to come down the road, but she could have no confidence in it. She had learned by now that nothing was going to help. But when she heard Jesus was coming, she thought, "If I just touch his clothes, I will be healed." Not "I might be healed." This woman was confident because she knew Jesus.

This nameless woman is a teacher of the fear of the Lord. She first listened to Jesus and saw what he did. Undoubtedly she was amazed by what she heard and saw. But her amazement led her to a confidence that Jesus was the Messiah, the Son of God.

What about you? When you read about these events, are you astonished, or are they just another Sunday school lesson? Allow this woman to let you see the Son of God in a new way, bigger than before. Then let her teach you further: "Don't just stand there with your mouth open. Believe!" Awe is good, but awe must lead us to faith, and faith must lead to action.

The Fear of the Lord: "Fear Not"

Continuing in the book of amazement, Mark tells another story where people were in awe. But it was the kind of awe where the witnesses could do nothing but stand there with their mouths open. The event was the Transfiguration, when Jesus gave a visual glimpse of his divine splendor. Peter was just standing there with his mouth open. But Jesus knew that the seeds of faith in Peter's life would soon yield great fruit, so he let Peter simply be amazed.

The Transfiguration is not unprecedented in Scripture. For example, Samson's parents witnessed a similar event (Judg. 13). They, however, had the usual reaction: "We are doomed to die! We have seen God!" Peter's reaction was unique.

Why Jesus took only Peter, James, and John, we don't know. But we do know that Jesus was giving them a gift that they would remember throughout their ministries. The disciples were reminded that the one who lived with them was God in the flesh. The gift was an advanced course in the fear of the Lord.

His face shone like the sun. His clothes became dazzling white, whiter than anyone could bleach them, as bright as a flash of lightning. And there appeared Elijah and Moses, who were talking with Jesus. They spoke about his departure, which he was about to bring to fulfillment at Jerusalem. (Matt. 17:1–3; Mark 9:1–4; Luke 9:28–31)

Of course, the disciples were frightened. They were roused out of sleep by this awesome display of glory. But Peter's response was certainly unique in all of Scripture. Why did he ever suggest that they put up three tabernacles—one for Jesus, one for Moses, and one for Elijah? I'm sure he had his reasons, but it isn't worth trying to understand, because the book of Mark gives the real reason. In one of the more humorous editorial remarks in the Bible, Mark explains Peter's silliness: "He did not know what to say, they were so frightened" (Mark 9:6). Most people are silent in their awe. Peter had to say something. God, graciously, interrupted.

> *While he was speaking a cloud appeared and enveloped Jesus and the three disciples, and a voice came from the cloud. "This is my son, whom I love. Listen to him!" When the disciples heard this, they fell to the ground, terrified. But Jesus came and touched them. "Get up," he said. "Don't be afraid." When they looked up, they saw no one except Jesus. (Matt. 17:5–8; Mark 9:7–8; Luke 9:34–35)*

Jesus, the great shepherd, whose holy love is as awesome as his power, said, "Don't be afraid." The words were familiar. The disciples knew them from Moses and Joshua, but they were never more meaningful. Again, Jesus invites us to come near and know him.

The Fear of the Lord and the Gospel

All this was leading up to the death and resurrection of Jesus. It is good to be amazed at everything in the Bible, but this is where holy love and holy justice are one. As a result, our fear (reverence, faith) should always end at the gospel.

Holy love—he was like a sheep going to the slaughter, instead of us. "While we were still sinners [enemies], Christ died for us."

Holy justice—the penalty for sin is the removal of the very presence of God. "My God, my God, why have you forsaken me?"

His death should provoke godly fear in us. There is no other act that encompasses such holy love and holy justice.

Such a death did lead to amazement, but you may be surprised at *who* was amazed. Mark mentions a number of women who were watching, but he doesn't offer their response. He doesn't mention any disciples. The only personal response to Jesus' death mentioned in the book of Mark was that of a Roman centurion. We don't know what he witnessed of the ministry of Jesus. He may have witnessed only his death. But what he says is truly remarkable. It sounds like awe that extends to faith.

> *And when the centurion, who stood there in front of Jesus, heard his cry and saw how he died, he said, "Surely this man was the Son of God!" (Mark 15:39)*

Jesus had done and said things that left the crowds amazed. After a while, the crowds were amazed just at the sight of him. But the most astounding comment in this book of amazement is perhaps that of the centurion, and all he seemed to be doing was witnessing the deaths of three enemies of Rome.

I have read about the deaths of many famous men and women. Some people went raging into death either by taking their own lives or shaking their fists at God. Others were surrounded by friends and students, and witnesses remarked how peacefully and calmly they died. But I have never read a record of someone being awed by a person's death.

Jesus gave no sermons from the cross, and he did no apparent miracles. He just died, and the centurion knew beyond any doubt that Jesus was the Son of God.

Mark then testifies to the fact that Jesus conquered death. His succinct report makes it sound almost anticlimactic, as if he was saying, "Of course, having heard Jesus testify of himself and validate his testimony with words and deeds, we knew that death could never contain him. After all, Jesus is the Holy One who is above death, not below it." But Mark can't help but record one more response of amazement. It is probable that his epistle ends with these words.

> *Trembling and bewildered, the women went out and fled from the tomb. They said nothing to anyone, because they were afraid. (Mark 16:8)*

Their fear (being afraid) and bewilderment would soon turn to fear (reverential obedience or worship) and confidence.

All these biblical examples point to the same conclusions: The triune God delights in showing us his grandeur and holiness, and we should never be satisfied with our present knowledge of him. So aspire to the fear of the Lord. Such a desire will certainly be satisfied as we pray,

> *Lord, teach your church to fear you. Your grace is not always amazing to us. We are slow to hate our sin. We are more concerned with what someone thinks about our appearance than we are about reverential obedience before you. We want to delight in fear. We want to treasure it and give it to the next generation. Amen.*

For Further Thought

The key to learning the fear of the Lord is to stay in Scripture. When you are in the Scripture, pray that God would teach you that he is the Holy One.

1. Review the creation psalms: Psalms 8; 19; 29; 65; 104.
2. Meditate on the enthronement psalms: e.g., Psalm 95–97; 99.

3. Memorize Psalm 139. It states that God's providence is so extensive it goes into all the details of our lives.

4. Go through a hymn book and highlight songs that express God's majesty and holiness.

5. Read the book of Habakkuk. It is similar to Job in that God directly addresses a man who had questions about what God was doing. All the questions were resolved when Habakkuk was schooled in the fear of the Lord.

6. Read *The Holiness of God,* by R. C. Sproul (Wheaton, Ill.: Tyndale House, 1985).

7. Review the New Testament passages on hell. Along with the ones mentioned in this chapter, you could consider 2 Thessalonians 1:5–10; 2 Peter 2:6; and Revelation 14:9–11. Be certain to talk with other people in your church about your meditations. Bless them with what God is teaching you, and listen to what God has taught them.

8. Begin a "fear of the Lord" or "knowing God" prayer group.

9. Take time to confess your fear of people and lack of fear of the Lord.

CHAPTER

BIBLICALLY EXAMINE YOUR FELT NEEDS

Fear the LORD, you his saints, for those who fear him lack nothing.   *—Psalm 34:9*

WHEN you spend time in the throne room of God, it puts things in perspective. The opinions of others are less important, and even our opinions of ourselves seem less important. Maybe that is all we need. Daily stops in the court of the Lord cure the fear of man. But what if you still feel like your needs have not been met? What if self-esteem remains a crippling concern? The fear of the Lord is the heart of the biblical treatment for the fear of people, but it is not the only treatment. Liberation from the fear of man has three components: we must have a biblically informed knowledge of God, other people, and ourselves. In this chapter, we will look more closely at what God says about ourselves and our needs.

STEP 5   *Examine where your desires have been too big. When we fear people, people are big, our desires are even bigger, and God is small.*

The question is this: What is our basic, God-given shape or identity? The prevailing notion is that we are created as psychologically needy. You can find it in bookstores, secular and Christian. You can hear it in counseling offices. And it is part of casual conversation in both the church and the world.

➤ "If only my husband would encourage me more."

➤ "If only my wife would respect me."

➤ "If only my children would obey me."

➤ "If only he [she] would show some interest in me."

➤ "If only my parents would give me more independence."

Can you hear it? The love cup lives. "Fill me with _____, then I will be happy." We tend to see ourselves as people who need something from somebody if we are going to change.

The Popular View of People

Pieced together, a popular view of the person looks like this:

1. Our basic shape is that of a receptacle—a cup—that holds psychic needs.

2. We have a long list of psychic needs, but these needs tend to cluster around the basic needs for love and significance.

3. When these needs are not met, we are in a deficit, and so we feel empty.

4. We must be careful who fills these needs. Either we can look to people, or we can look to Christ.

What Are Needs?

As we look at these four ideas, a natural place to begin decoding our view of ourselves is with our understanding of our own needs. What would you say that you really need? Your answers will get to the heart of your view of yourself.

The answer is easy for me. I need my wife to love me. I need to have a sense that I contribute at work. I need my children to obey me, especially when other people are at our house. I need money, of course. I think that's about it—for now.

How would you answer the question? One way would be to ask another question: "What do you mean by 'need'?" The word certainly can have different shades of meaning. If you were lost in the desert and dying of thirst, you would answer "water." If your pastor asked the question during a sermon, and especially if he said, "What do you *really* need?," then you would probably say, "Jesus." If, however, somebody asked you the question over a cup of coffee, the answer would be anybody's guess: respect, love, understanding, someone who listens, self-esteem, obedient kids, safety, control, excitement—the list is limited only by human imagination and desires.

Welcome to the word "need," one of the more confusing terms in the English language. Everybody uses it, but it can express ideas that are completely unrelated. For example, "I need a vacation" is a cultural way of saying that I am getting tired of the day-to-day grind of work. "I need my wife's respect" reveals a belief that I will experience a psychological deficit if my wife doesn't service this perceived psychic necessity. "I need water" is a way of expressing a true biological need that, when denied, will actually lead to poor health or death. "I need sex" typically expresses a lustful heart, but the heart fools itself into thinking that it is only asking for a biological necessity.

Some meanings are almost neutral: a wife says to her husband, "We need a gallon of milk and a loaf of bread." Other meanings are laden with complications: the husband retorts, "I need you to get off my case." Among all these uses of the word "need," there are three different clusters of meaning: biological needs, spiritual needs, and psychological needs.

Biological needs. Biological needs are pretty straightforward. We need food, water, and shelter; otherwise, we die. This is a common use of the word "need" in the Scriptures. Jesus exhorts us not to worry about what we will eat, or drink, or wear, because "your heavenly Father knows that you need them" (Matt. 6:32).

This category has become confusing only recently. For example, "I need a beer" has been migrating into this category for decades. Alcohol is no longer the satisfier of a desire that results from experience, practice, and lust; rather, the "need" is perceived as a biological drive that is nearly irresistible. Or consider the popular "I need sex." When this is elbowed out of the category of desire and lust into the biological, the assumption is that sex is a biological need, nearly identical to food and water. The reasoning is that since it is a biological need, sexual self-control is unnatural, and the only option is to practice "safe" sex. Abstinence, therefore, is both old-fashioned and biologically untenable.

Spiritual needs. A second use of the word "need" is spiritual need. Apart from Jesus, we are desperate, needy people. We are dead in our sins, we are enemies of God, we stand condemned before him, we are enslaved by Satan and our own desires, and we are hopelessly unable to remedy our situation or please God. These clearly are our most profound needs.

Yet our triune God does not leave us alone. Jesus has become our need-meeter. In Jesus, he makes us alive, he reconciles us to himself and calls us friends, he legally pardons us, and he redeems us from the bondage of sin and Satan. According to Scripture, Jesus meets all our needs for life and godliness (2 Peter 1:3).

Psychological needs. Now it gets tricky. The borders for the third category are more difficult to find. These are called psychological needs. The list of psychological needs can be a long one, but they typically have to do with what we want in relationships: significance, acceptance, respect, admiration, love, belonging, meaning, and so on. Some people collapse this long list into one: the need for love.

In the United States, a need for love is typically assumed to be as basic to human nature as biological needs and spiritual needs. It can be just as strong as our biological needs to eat and sleep.[1] As already noted in chapter 5, books such as *Love Is a Choice* state that we have a "God-given need to be loved that is born into every human infant. It is a legitimate need that must be met from cradle to grave. If children are deprived of love—if that primal need for love is not met—they carry the scars for life."[2] But there are two questions that are rarely asked about this need for love. First, while we all agree that love is a universal human *desire,* how do we justify elevating desire to God-given *need?* There is a significant difference between the two words. Second, and perhaps more importantly, what is the purpose of having this need met?

The answer to the first question is usually, "God created us in his image and said that it is not good for us to be alone. Therefore we need people." This makes biblical sense. There is a way in which we need people. But this leaves the second question: What, according to the category of psychological needs, do we need people for? According to the category of spiritual needs, we need people to warn us about the deceitfulness of sin, to point us to the love of Jesus, to

1 Tom Whiteman and Randy Petersen, *Love Gone Wrong* (Nashville: Nelson, 1994), 90.
2 Robert Hemfelt, Frank Minirth, and Paul Meier, *Love Is a Choice* (Nashville: Nelson), 34.

help carry our burdens, and for many other things. What about the category of psychological needs?

Although this question is rarely asked, the answer is usually apparent in the many books that assume psychological needs. According to the popular thinking, these needs must be met so that we can reach our potential and have happiness, psychological stability, and self-esteem. Put less technically, *our psychological needs must be filled in order for us to feel good about ourselves.*

Biological needs	Needed for physical life	Food, water, clothes, shelter
Spiritual needs	Needed for spiritual life, faith, obedience ...	Forgiveness of sins, adoption, sanctification, glorification
Psychological needs	Needed for happiness and acceptance ...	Love, significance, security, and self-esteem ...

Figure 1. Popular Uses of the Word Need

We know that we are created to live in relationship with other people, and in these relationships we are to love, encourage, and comfort each other, but is the purpose of these relationships to bolster our self-esteem? At first glance the Scripture can support the idea that we have a need *to show love* to others, but it is more difficult to find Scripture that says we have a God-given need to receive love so that we can feel better about ourselves. Where does the Bible talk about these needs?

Needs: An Experience in Search of a Proof Text

When left only partially defined, psychological needs seemed quite normal, but now, with their goal revealed, these particular needs seem somewhat self-centered, and biblical support for them may be hard to find. Thoughtful people, however, have found these needs in Scripture. They propose that God-given needs can be found in either of two prominent biblical categories: the person-as-body-soul-spirit, and the person-as-created-in-the-image-of-God. Perhaps you weren't expecting a theological excursion on the path to dealing with the fear of other people, but our lives proceed out of our theology—our understanding of God and ourselves. Therefore, it is essential that we examine these theological assumptions.

The person as three substances. The tripartite view of the person—meaning that we are body, soul, and spirit—was the first biblical category asked to carry the freight of psychological needs. The popular idea is that the physical body has physical needs, the soul has psychological needs, and the spirit has spiritual needs. Accordingly, the person with physical needs goes to a physician, the person with psychological needs goes to a psychologist or counselor, and the person with spiritual needs goes to a pastor.

This basic formula, however, as simple and biblical as it appears, has some unintended implications. It has essentially given secular psychology permission to shape one-third of the person. "Soul" becomes a blank category to be filled with speculative psychological theories. As medicine has contributed many details to the category of the body, so secular psychology can now contribute to (or completely flesh out) our understanding of the soul. And somehow, the need for careful biblical analysis of what we say about it seems to slip by us; it appears that we have already done this by naming the category "soul." However, we must first ask if we even *have* a soul that is clearly distinct from the spirit.

The tripartite view of the person exists because there are different shades of meaning for spirit and soul. Like most words, these two have fuzzy boundaries. They are not technical words such as "electron," but are more like the word "need," deriving much of their meaning from their context. The question, however, is whether these shades of meaning are sufficient to suggest that spirit and soul are two distinct created substances. Or, are spirit and soul (like "heart," "mind," "conscience") slightly different perspectives on the one, immaterial inner person (2 Cor. 4:16)?

A number of biblical passages suggest that the person is best understood as two substances—physical and spiritual—which belong together although they can be separated by death. From this vantage point, the terms "spirit" and "soul" emphasize different aspects of the same substance. They are essentially interchangeable, but offer different perspectives on the immaterial person. For example, Matthew 10:28 suggests that the person is two substances, material body and immaterial soul: "Do not be afraid of those who kill the body [material substance] but cannot kill the soul [immaterial substance]." First Corinthians 7:34 also suggests that we are two substances—material and immaterial—but they are referred to as body and spirit rather than body and soul. James 2:26 is consistent with this duality and refers to it using "body" and "spirit": "the body without the spirit is dead."

The two passages most frequently cited for the three-part or trichotomist view of the person are Hebrews 4:12 and 1 Thessalonians 5:23. Hebrews 4:12 states, "The word of God is living and active. Sharper than any double-edged sword, it penetrates even to dividing soul and spirit, joints and marrow; it judges the thoughts and attitudes of the heart." Some think this refers to a dissection of the parts of the person. That is, the Word of God can separate soul from spirit; therefore, they are two separate substances that are part of the whole person. However, if the intent of the passage is to speak technically about the parts of the person, then there are at least *four* substances that make up the whole person: the soul, spirit, body (joints and marrow), and heart (with the heart further divided into thoughts and attitudes). It is more likely that the passage suggests that God's Word penetrates the indivisible aspect of the person. It goes to the very depths of the person's being. It goes *within* the substance of the person, not *between,* as if it were slicing us up into neat pieces. The fact that the inner person is referred to as soul, spirit, and heart is a common poetic means of emphasizing that the whole person is involved. For example, Mark 12:30 indicates that we are to "love the Lord your God with all your heart and with all your soul and with all your mind and with all your strength." The accumulation of terms is used to express completeness. It is a dramatic way of emphasizing that loving God is a response of the entire person.

The most the Bible can say about the distinction between soul and spirit is that "soul" emphasizes the person in a weak, earthly existence and "spirit" highlights the fact that our life is derived from God. Neither term suggests that we were created with a distinct category called psychological needs. Instead, they are overlapping words that refer to the inner person, the immaterial aspect of humanness, or the person who lives before the Holy God.

So we can't find psychological needs here.

The image of God in man. The other category that is used as the biblical background for psychological needs is the image of God in man.

> *So God created man in his own image,*
> *in the image of God he created him;*
> *male and female he created them. (Gen. 1:27)*

This is the core doctrine for understanding the person. It is so important that every Bible student should have a quick definition of what it means and the difference it makes to be created in God's image. Are psychological needs found here? If not, then they are not God-given needs.

Most Christians would suggest that the image of God in man has something to do with what is similar between God and man. According to psychological-need theory, what is similar is that both God and man have a deep longing for relationship (or love). This longing is defined as a subjective experience that is deeper than emotion. It is a *passion* for relationship. For God, this means that he

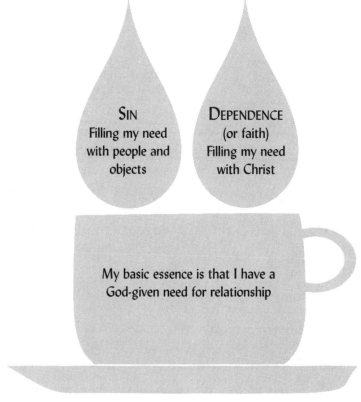

Figure 2. The Psychological-Needs Model

exists in joyous relationship with himself—Father, Son, Holy Spirit. It also means that God has a longing for restoration of relationship with his children.[3]

Therefore, according to this theory, the essence of image-bearing is that "we all long for what God designed us to enjoy: tension-free relationships filled with deep, loving acceptance and with opportunities to make a difference to someone else."[4] "Each of us fervently wants someone to see us exactly as we are, warts and all, and still accept us."[5] Without this longing fulfilled, we are empty cups.

How will I deal with my longings? then becomes the fundamental question of human existence. According to the theory, we answer this question in one of two ways. We either act independently of God and look to fill ourselves with other objects or people, or we look to Christ and find relationship needs met in him (Figure 2).

When this model is evaluated by our experience, it seems to fit perfectly. Like any other influential model, this model tends to "work." It seems self-evident. But is it self-evident because of the cultural smog or because of the clear teaching of Scripture?

Notice one of its implications about God. There is no doubt that God loves his people, but the perspective of God's "longings" raises some troubling questions. Doesn't "longing" sound like "desperately want" or "need"? Doesn't it suggest that God is incomplete without relationship with us? Doesn't it suggest that God himself has a deficit that must be filled by us? The truth is that God loves us because of his own sovereign pleasure and for the sake of his own glory. His glory is even greater when we realize that he *didn't need* to love us.

---

3 Larry Crabb, *Understanding People* (Grand Rapids: Zondervan, 1976), 94.
4 Larry Crabb, *Inside Out* (Colorado Springs: NavPress, 1991), 53–54.
5 Crabb, *Understanding People*, 112.

Also notice what a need-based theory suggests about ourselves. It says that we have a longings problem that is at least as deep as our sin problem. In practice this means that if a pastor treats a person's gossip as sin, the gossiper can say that the counsel is superficial. "The pastor didn't get the real heart of my problem. My problem is that I need relationship. I am lonely." While it may be true that the gossiper desperately wants a relationship, it is also true that the deepest, most profound explanation for her gossip is her own sin. Her gossip is an expression of a heart that screams, *"I want."* It is a commitment to self and against God. The cause of sin is . . . sin. To assume that loneliness is the *real* core of the problem is to minimize the against-God nature of sin and to encourage blame-shifting.

If we think that sin is in any way superficial, then we do not understand the true nature of sin.

When psychological needs, rather than sin, are seen as our primary problem, not only is our self-understanding affected, but the gospel itself is changed. A needs theory suggests that the gospel is, most deeply, intended to meet psychological needs. In other words, the gospel is aimed at our self-esteem problem. It is aimed at our tendency to dwell on our failures. It is intended to be a statement of God's love saying that "God doesn't make junk."

This sounds good to us, but it is not the gospel. The good news of Jesus is not intended to make us feel good about ourselves. Instead, the good news humbles us. In Isaiah 6, for example, the presence of God first destroyed Isaiah's view of himself, then it cleansed him and liberated him from himself and his own sinful desires. After his symbolic cleansing and liberation, Isaiah was freed to be less concerned about himself and more concerned about the plan of God.

Jesus did not die to increase our self-esteem. Rather, Jesus died to bring glory to the Father by redeeming people from the curse of sin. Of course, the cross has many benefits, one being that we are no longer cast out of the presence of God and we have intimacy with the Holy One. But the cross deals with our sin problem, our *spiritual* need.

Human relationships, too, are affected by this needs theology. For example, marriage becomes mutual need-meeting. At first glance, this seems to fit the experience of marriage, and it also seems to square with Scripture's view of love. People are commanded to love because (from this perspective) we need love. Is it possible, however, that we are called to love not because other people are empty and need love (to feel better about themselves) but because love is the way in which we imitate Christ and bring glory to God?

Notice what happens when a husband needs love, in the form of respect, from his wife. His thinking is that God made him with this need, and his wife is obligated to fill it—God himself commanded her. As a result, he believes that he is owed respect, and he has a right to be angry when his wife doesn't fill this need.

When we have a *desire* for respect and we don't receive it, we are hurt. If we have a *need* for respect, we are devastated or angry.

God's commands to love, listen, bear burdens, or wash feet do not imply that we have psychological needs for these things. Perhaps we can say that we need to *give* them, but Scripture doesn't suggest that we must have them to make us feel better about ourselves. Instead, Scripture questions the whole purpose of psychological needs. It talks about denying self rather than feeling better about ourselves. It talks about pride, not a need for higher self-esteem. Also, it is faulty logic to draw a connection between God's commands and our "need" to receive what is commanded. If you applied that logic to the command to "consider others better than yourselves" (Phil. 2:3), you would reach a conclusion that is clearly wrong. You would conclude that since others are commanded to do this, you have a God-given need to be more important than other people!

Where Do Psychological Needs Come From?

How, then, are we to understand these felt needs biblically? Where can we find them in Scripture? There is no clear evidence that they are a distinct part of our God-given nature, yet they are real. If the Bible was mute on these, it would be silent on a prominent, nearly universal human experience.

Instead of looking for this concept at the time of creation, when we were created in the image of God, perhaps we should look at the time *after* Adam's sin. After the fall into sin, people remained image-bearers, but Adam's disobedience brought fundamental changes to our ability to reflect God's image. The direction of the human heart became oriented not toward God but toward self. In the garden, man began repeating a mantra that will persist until Jesus returns. Adam said, *"I want."* "I want glory for myself rather than giving all glory to God." "I love my own desires rather than loving God." This came to be known as covetousness, lust, or idolatry.

Is it possible that the *"I want"* of Adam is the first expression of psychological needs? Is it possible that psychological yearnings come when we refuse to love God and receive his love? Wasn't it with Adam that the momentum of human life started moving inward toward the desires of the self, rather than outward, toward a desire to know and do the will of God?

This is not to say that taking delight in being loved was the original sin. Certainly not. Since we were forged by The Lover, we *should* delight in loving and in being loved. It would be inhuman *not* to delight in love. It would also be inhuman if we didn't hurt deeply when rejected or sinned against by others. The problem is not that we desire love, the problem is *how much* we desire it or *for what purpose* we desire it. Do we desire it so much that it overshadows our desire to be imitators of God? Do we desire it for our own pleasure or for God's glory?

Longings have much in common with lust. They start out good (a desire to be loved) and end up enslaving us. To elevate our desire for love, impact, and other pleasures to the point where they become needs or longings is to sinfully exalt desire so that it becomes a delirium of desire. It is to yell out, *"I want!" "I must have!" "My desires are the basic building blocks of my world!"*

Consider the times when you have felt controlled by other people—times they "made you" angry or depressed. Now look underneath that bondage. How would you complete the sentence "I need _____" or "I long for _____"? Could it be more accurately phrased, *"I want"* _____ [love, security, significance, power] and I am not getting it!" *"I demand* _____!" *"I insist on* _____!" or, *"I can't function/live/obey without* _____!"

This explains why Christ is sometimes not enough for us. If I stand before him as a cup waiting to be filled with psychological satisfaction, I will never feel quite full. Why? First, because my lusts are boundless; by their very nature, they can't be filled. Second, because Jesus does not intend to satisfy my selfish desires. Instead, he intends to *break* the cup of psychological need (lusts), not fill it.

A Christian movie portrayed a teenager being wooed to Christ with the promise of better grades upon conversion. Trust Christ, get better grades—sounds great! Just add a few other perks like money, an attractive date, and the family car, and every teenager will convert. But isn't that just appealing to lusts rather than offering deliverance and forgiveness from them? Israelite evangelism never suggested that neighboring idolaters start worshipping the true God because Yahweh would give better crops than their idols. Instead, people were, and are, called to turn from their idols because idolatry is against God.

To look to Christ to meet our perceived psychological needs is to Christianize our lusts. We are asking God to give us what we want, *so we can feel better about ourselves,* or so we can have more happiness, not holiness, in our lives.

This reminds us that one of the shapes we have is that of sinners. *Sinner* is no longer our primary shape or identity, but it is an identity we still retain. Someday we will be a *thoroughly* beautiful bride, but until that day we remain sinners who sin.

This resident *"I want"* is more than something we occasionally do. It is woven into the fabric of our lives in such a way that it is part of who we are. For example, are you sinless when you sleep? I'll be even more specific. Are you sinless when you sleep and are not having any dreams? The biblical answer is clearly no. It is like asking me, "Are you still 'Ed' when you sleep?" "Sinner" is a present-tense description of everyone, including those who have put their faith in Christ. Of course, those who have called Jesus "Lord" are justified, meaning that they are no longer guilty. Also, they have been given the Spirit, which makes them slaves to Christ rather than to sin. But we all are still sinners. Perfection awaits eternity.

As sinners who sin, we are in debt to a holy God. We owe him perfect allegiance, glory, praise, and honor, but we have paid him nothing because we are thoroughly destitute. Therefore, one of our deepest needs is forgiveness. "Forgive us our debts," we pray, and God, in Christ, forgives our debt (Matt. 6:12).

Now we are *really* in God's debt, but it is not a debt that leaves us ashamed. We *were* in his debt because of our sin, and we were people in shame. Now, we *are* in his debt because of his forgiveness, and we are filled with gratitude. Yet even this is not the full extent of our present debt. Our Heavenly Father has also made us children and heirs. He has given us a new family and new identity. Furthermore, this is only the deposit guaranteeing what he has prepared for us. He has seated us in heavenly places—in the very throne room of God—and given us the privilege of abiding with him forever.

He has canceled our debt but didn't leave us debt-free beggars. He also made us rich. *That* is a debt that can lead us into rejoicing.

Now I understand what held me in the fear of man, even though I knew the gospel well. Not only did I need to grow in the fear of the Lord; I also needed to repent. My felt needs, desires, or lusts were big. They were so big that I looked to everybody to fill them, both God and other people. I feared other people because people were big, *my desires were even bigger,* and God was small.

The main reason why there is an epidemic of emptiness is that *we* have created and multiplied our needs, not God.[6]

For Further Thought

This chapter has uncovered a missing link in the way we often deal with being controlled by people: We forget that we must repent of our self-centered desires. Without repentance, our desires remain the focal point instead of God's glory.

Take time and consider how many of your "psychological needs" have really been wants and demands in disguise.

6 Lusts are not the only reason for emptiness. Another explanation for emptiness arises out of the fact that we are living in a sinful world where we are sinned against, and we are living in a world that is under the curse. For example, if your spouse died, you would feel empty. You should feel empty. Something beautiful has been removed from life. There is a great sense of loss. This emptiness, however, is the result of the curse and death etching themselves on our psyche, and not the result of being created with psychological longings.

C H A P T E R

Know Your Real Needs

NOW let's go back to the question, Who are we? We have considered how some of our felt needs are *not* part of the image of God in us, but we have not discussed what *is* the image of God in us. What are the biblical alternatives to people-as-empty-cups?

Since the image of God in man has to do with our likeness or similarity to God (Gen. 3:5), the starting point should be, "Who is God?" Any doctrine of the image of God must travel easily and frequently between the knowledge of God and the knowledge of ourselves. Only after we gain a right understanding of God can we begin to ask, "Who is the person?"

Who Is God and What Are His "Needs"?

God and his kingdom are, simply put, about God—the triune God, the Holy One of Israel. What are the triune God's needs? He has no needs. He is completely fulfilled. The Father loves the Son. The Son is ecstatic about the Father and wants nothing but the Father's will. God's greatest pleasure is himself. [1] This may sound

---

1 A helpful discussion of this theme can be found in John Piper's, *The Pleasures of God.*

strange at first, but how could we expect God to be consumed with anything less than his own perfect, holy being? For God to be consumed with anything else would be idolatrous. It would be exalting the creature above the Creator. God's goal is to exalt himself and his own glory. He intends to magnify his great name. "For from him and through him and to him are all things. To him be glory forever" (Rom. 11:36).

Notice that a difference has already arisen between this perspective and the new need psychology. In need psychology, the natural reason to praise God is for what he has done for *me*. This is okay, but it doesn't go far enough. From the Bible's perspective, God deserves praise *simply because he is God*. The natural focal point for our thoughts is not our own deep longings but the immeasurably great "God of glory" (Acts 7:2), the Holy One of Israel who reigns. Rightly seen and understood, this glory is all-consuming. The Israelites did not break out into song because their psychological longings had been fulfilled; they exalted God simply because he is exalted (Ex. 15:11): "Who among the gods is like you, O LORD? Who is like you—majestic in holiness, awesome in glory, working wonders?" In reciting this, their *real* needs were being satisfied.

Glory, honor, radiance, beauty, splendor, majesty—all these are interchangeable terms for God's greatness. "Holiness" is the word that wraps them together.

We have already discussed how God's holiness is expressed in his love and justice. Now let's go one step further. God's love and justice are expressed in scores of very concrete pictures or *images* that we can imitate. For example, the Holy One is the loving bridegroom who expects a spotless bride. He is the feast-giver who invites everyone to the feast, but expects attendees to wear the garment given them. He is a loving redeemer who redeems Zion with justice (Isa. 1:27). He is the judge over all the earth, yet his own

Son becomes the advocate and representative for his inglorious people. He is the father, mother, submissive son, suffering servant, friend, shepherd, physician, meaning-maker, creator, and potter. He is the rock and fortress. Indeed, images or pictures of God are everywhere in the Bible, and each picture is an expression of his holiness.

These concrete "snapshots" that God gives us of himself are not just God's way of accommodating himself to human language. God isn't using our understanding of servants to suggest that he is like a servant. No, God is *the* servant, *the* husband, *the* father, *the* brother, and *the* friend. Anything in the created world that bears a resemblance to these descriptions of God is simply God's glory spilling into creation and into creatures. Whenever you see these albeit distorted images in other people, they are a faint reflection of the original. I am a father because God is a father. I am a worker because God is the original worker.

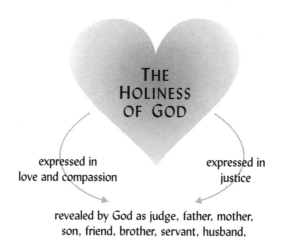

Figure 1. Our God: The Holy One

All these pictures merge into one when you witness the glory or holiness in Jesus Christ, the ultimate image of God's glory (Heb. 1:3). "We have seen his glory, the glory of the One and Only, who came from the Father, full of grace and truth" (John 1:14). He is called "the Holy One of God" (Mark 1:24; John 6:69). His passion, as you would expect, was the glory of the Father. For example, before his crucifixion his prayer was "Father, glorify your name" (John 12:28). In his prayer immediately before his arrest, Jesus prayed to his "Holy Father" (John 17:11) and "Righteous Father" (John 17:25) that the Father would glorify Jesus so that Jesus in turn may glorify the Father. The deepest desire on Jesus' heart was the glory of his Holy Father, and this desire was expressed in Jesus' love and justice. This is the One to fix your eyes on as you seek to be an image-bearer of the most high God.

Who Are We?

Armed with an understanding of God, the question "Who is the person?" becomes fairly straightforward. How are people similar to the Creator God? The object of God's greatest affections is God himself: the Father, Son, and Spirit. He wants his glorious holiness to fill the earth. Therefore, our prayer should be "Hallowed be your name." People are most similar to God when he is the object of their affection. People should delight in God, as he does in himself. We are to make his name famous or hallowed throughout the world; we are to declare the coming of his glorious kingdom. As the Westminster Catechism says, "The chief end of man is to glorify God and enjoy him [or delight in him] forever" (Q. 1).(Figure 2.)

Instead of the image of God in human beings taking the form of a love cup or a hollow core of longings, the image is more accurately that of Moses literally reflecting the glory of God (Ex. 34:29–32), like the moon reflecting the light of the sun. Moses was radiant

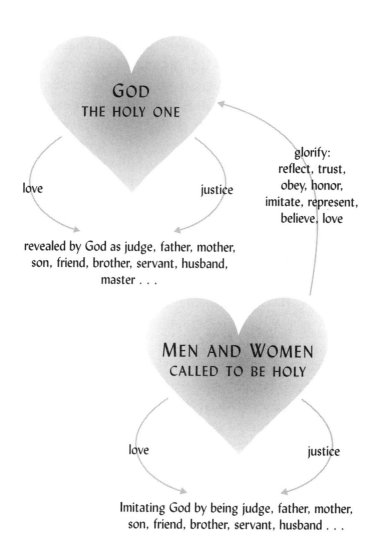

love   justice

glorify:
reflect, trust,
obey, honor,
imitate, represent,
believe, love

revealed by God as judge, father, mother,
son, friend, brother, servant, husband,
master . . .

love   justice

Imitating God by being judge, father, mother,
son, friend, brother, servant, husband . . .

Figure 2. The Person (and the Church): Reflecting God's Glory

because he was invited into the presence of the Lord and both
witnessed God's glory-holiness and was protected from it.

As marvelous as this seems, God has made us, his renewed

image-bearers, even more glorious than Moses. God's people still must have his presence to be his image-bearers, but his presence is no longer limited to occasional theophanies or dependent on the functioning tabernacle. Today, the way God's people come into his presence is by faith. By faith, we have the indwelling glory of the Spirit. As a result, instead of the glory eventually fading, we can grow to be even more radiant. "And we, who with unveiled faces all reflect the Lord's glory, are being transformed into his likeness with ever-increasing glory, which comes from the Lord, who is the Spirit" (2 Cor. 3:18).

This means that the essence of imaging God is to rejoice in God's presence, to love him above all else, and to live for his glory, not our own. The most basic question of human existence becomes "How can I bring glory to God?"—not "How will God meet my psychological longings?" These differences create very different tugs on our hearts: one constantly pulls us outward toward God, the other first pulls inward toward ourselves.

Furthermore, instead of the image of God being a place inside you—a hollow core that is passive and easily damaged—the image-as-bringing-glory-to-God is found in the way we live. It suggests that our hearts are always active, either in bringing glory to God or to self. In this sense, the image of God in man is a verb. It is not just who we are; it is what we do. Faith, the means by which we image God, is expressed in the way we live, as are its many synonyms, such as imitating God (Eph. 5:1), representing God (2 Cor. 5:20), mirroring or reflecting the glory of God (Ex. 34:29–35), loving God, and living according to his will.

Ultimately, the awesome responsibility and glorious privilege of image-bearing is expressed in simple acts of obedience that have eternal implications. Imaging God is loving him and loving your neighbor. In the same way that God's holy love and justice are manifested in concrete acts, so should ours be. Wherever you find faith and trust, you will find people imaging God:

➤ In meeting with God's people, for God's glory.

➤ In praying for each other and the world, for God's glory.

➤ In listening to a spouse rather than being defensive, for God's glory.

➤ In going to work, for God's glory.

➤ In enjoying marital sexuality, for God's glory.

➤ In parenting, for God's glory.

This understanding of God's holiness and our design as image-bearers yields a vast number of alternatives to the love cup. They reside on every page of the Bible. You can find them in the way God talks about us, his Son, and even himself. Certainly, that does not mean that we are to be almighty as God is almighty; there are some qualities of God that are not shared by his creatures. Yet there are many ways that God reveals himself that are patterns for us to follow. Let's look at some examples.

You Are a Priest

You already know that you are a latter-day Moses who lives in the presence of the Lord. As a result, your face shines with the presence of Jesus. This is another way of saying that you are God's priests. God's people are "a chosen people, a royal priesthood, a holy nation, a people belonging to God" (1 Peter 2:9). This is a God-given shape or image. It is also a shape that we witness in Jesus, who is the Great High Priest. Jesus is the High Priest; we too are priests as we imitate him.

Since this is who you are, you should know something about your history. The priests were called by God to represent him in a unique way as they served before God's tabernacle, his presence. The problem was that, like Adam and Eve, the priests were spiritually naked and ashamed before God. They needed God's covering to minister in his presence. Therefore, God made them garments that were nothing short of royal robes. These garments gave the wearer "dignity and honor" (Ex. 28:2).

The priestly garments had a handful of wonderful accessories. For example, the ephod was a beautiful piece of cloth that bore the names of the twelve tribes. It reminds us that we do not stand alone before the Lord, but we are in solidarity with other Christians. The breastpiece was also a skillfully crafted garment used to make godly decisions. It reminds us that all our decisions are done by consulting God's Word. The finishing touch, and perhaps most important because it covered the head, was the turban. A turban in itself is not that significant, other than that it reminds us of our need for God's thorough covering. But the engraved seal across the turban summarized the entire garment, as well as our lives. It said, "HOLY TO THE LORD" (Ex. 28:36). The priest belonged to God, represented God, was to be holy as God is holy, and lived to glorify God.

Through Christ, these garments are now available to all. They are given freely but must be worn. They are essential for giving glory to God. If you look at them closely, you will see that these priestly coverings double as the beautiful wedding garment that God's people wear at the consummation.

You Are a Christian

Modern priests are also called "Christians." This is perhaps a believer's most definitive shape or identity. It is another way of saying that we are God's family. This might not sound so dramatic in a day when our names don't have much significance. But in biblical times, the name often defined the person.

"Christian" certainly defines us. We have taken on Christ's name. We are his betrothed. Now our task is to make that name famous. We are heralds and ambassadors for Christ who implore others to be reconciled to God (2 Cor. 5:20). We are people who have received a new name through adoption. Furthermore, the adoption, no matter how much it makes us feel good, was not intended primarily for that purpose. In the New Testament, adoptions brought glory to the person who adopts, not the one who is adopted. Adoption brings glory to God.

Other Pictures of God's People

What are some other definitions that God has given us? Think as broadly as possible, and don't forget the more common pictures in Scripture. Any snapshot that God gives of himself is a possible shape for us. For example, as God's holiness is revealed in his fatherly love and discipling, our imitation can also be expressed in fathering. As his holiness is demonstrated in being a worker, so should ours. God has served us, and so we should imitate him and serve other people. Therefore, a Christian father who takes time to play soccer with his children is imaging the God who spends time with his people. A child who sets the table or cleans the dinner dishes out of obedience to Christ is imaging the servant God and thus glorifying him. Or a worker who does mundane work with the desire to serve Christ is imaging the Son who has worked on our behalf.

Here are just a few of the ways we imitate our God:

➤ As children (1 John 3:1).

➤ As slaves (Rom. 6:22).

➤ As friends (John 15:14).

➤ As fellow workers (Eph. 6:1).

➤ As brides (Rev. 21:3).

➤ As warriors (Eph. 6:10–18).

➤ As living stones (1 Peter 2:5).

➤ As evangelists, prophets, pastors, teachers (Eph. 4:11).

➤ As husbands (Isa. 54: 5).

All of these identities are ways we bring him glory.

What Do We Really Need?

So, other than forgiveness of sins, do we have any needs? Do we need relationships or not? The answer depends on what you mean by *need*. If we are talking about psychological needs, then no, we do not need relationships—with God or people—to fill our longings for significance and love.[2] That would be like saying that I need God to meet my need to feel great and important. Self-serving needs are not meant to be satisfied; they are meant to be put to death.

But what about the fact that Scripture commands us to love each other? Doesn't that mean we need love? Not necessarily. More accurately, it means that we need *to* love rather than that we have a

2 Some have suggested that the fact that infants need nurturing, such as hugs and other expressions of love, if they are going to thrive or even live, means that we have deep psychological longings. I think not. It is comparing apples and oranges. It is inaccurate to talk about an infant's longings and desires for relationship. It would be more accurate to say that we do need people in order to live. We are creatures who rely on other people every day. This, however, is different from putting our faith and trust in them.

psychological deficit that must be filled with love (and meaning, significance, and so on). Keep in mind that we have been created in the image of God. This means that we have been given gifts that enable us to represent and imitate him. Since we were created in love and are now sustained by God's patient love, we bring glory to God by imitating his persistent love. We love not because people have psychological deficits; we love because God first loved us.

The image of God in us is not about psychological need; it is about the abundance of gifts that God has given his people.

There is, however, a real sense in which we need other people. The fact that God created Adam *and* Eve indicates that the image of God in man could not be complete in any one nondivine person. Imaging God could not be done alone; it is done in partnership. His glory is too immense to be clearly reflected in any one creature. The image of God is corporate in that we all share in it. In a very practical sense, God's command to reproduce as a way to bring him glory is simply impossible for an individual. Therefore, God created male and female as his image-bearers.

The commands to reproduce and to subdue the earth are the forerunners of the New Testament's Great Commission, the command to preach Christ to the nations. Here again, this cannot be carried out by any one person. We need each other. For missionary work, we need farmers, truck drivers, engineers, builders, store owners, missionaries, mothers, fathers, pastors, Sunday school teachers, and janitors. The panoply of gifts is essential if the church is to function as God intended (1 Cor. 12:12–27). Image-bearers are not Lone Rangers.

Therefore, Scripture makes it clear that we *are* needy people.

1. We were created with biological needs. We need food and protection from harsh weather. We need God and, secondarily, other people to meet these needs.

2. We are sinners who have spiritual needs. Apart from the redeeming and sustaining work of Christ, we are spiritually dead. We need Jesus. We need to be taught of him and rebuked in love when we stray from him. Furthermore, as will be clarified in the next chapter, we need to know his immense love.

3. We were created as people with limited gifts and abilities. All the gifts of God are not contained in any one person. Therefore, we need other people in order to accomplish God's purposes and most accurately reflect his unlimited glory.

If there is any doubt about our true needs, we can examine some of the prayers of the Bible. Prayers are, after all, the calls of the needy heart. It is in the desperation of the prayers recorded in Scripture that we can see what we truly need. It is also in those prayers that we can find what God delights in giving to needy people.

This, then, is how you should pray:

> *"Our Father in heaven,*
> *hallowed be your name,*
> *your kingdom come,*
> *your will be done*
>   *on earth as it is in heaven.*
> *Give us today our daily bread.*
> *Forgive us our debts*
>   *as we also have forgiven our debtors.*
> *And lead us not into temptation,*
> *but deliver us from the evil one." (Matt. 6:9–13)*

The first petition of the Lord's Prayer is that God's name be hallowed, or regarded as holy. This is our greatest need; this is the *world's* greatest need. The prayer says nothing about psychological needs. It says nothing about personal happiness on earth! It *does* talk about our needs, but the needs are biological and spiritual, and even these needs are not primary. The greatest need of all humanity is that God be acknowledged and worshipped as the Holy One of Israel.

Not long before Jesus' death, he prayed to the Father. For Jesus, prayer was a daily occurrence, but this prayer was unique. First, it is recorded. Of the many times that Jesus prayed throughout the night, this is one of the few prayers we are privileged to overhear. Second, given that it is right before his crucifixion, it must be one of the most desperate prayers that Jesus prayed. As such, it gives us an idea of what was really important to him. We find out what he really needed.

It follows the model for prayer in Matthew 6.

> *Father, the time has come. Glorify your Son, that your Son may glorify you. . . . My prayer is not that you take them [those who will believe in Jesus] out of the world but that you protect them from the evil one. . . . Sanctify them by the truth. (John 17:1, 15, 17)*

There are two critical petitions: (1) that God be glorified, and (2) that God's people would grow in obedience. These were Jesus' two basic needs. They are ours as well.

One of the best-known prayers in the Epistles is the prayer of Paul in Ephesians 3.

> *For this reason I kneel before the Father, from whom his whole family in heaven and on earth derives its name. I pray that out of his glorious riches he may strengthen you with power through his Spirit in your inner being, so that Christ may dwell in your hearts through faith. And I pray that you, being rooted and established in love, may have power, together with all the*

*saints, to grasp how wide and long and high and deep is the
love of Christ, and to know this love that surpasses knowledge—that you may be filled to the measure of all the fullness
of God. (Eph. 3:14–19)*

Uh-oh, is this the return of the love cup? Is Paul praying that
our love cups would be filled? Perhaps we should skip this
prayer! But, then again, maybe we are reading psychological
needs into the prayer rather than really understanding what
Paul is praying.

There are two things we must remember about this passage.
First, Paul is using the metaphor of a cup, but it is not the cup of
psychological needs. It is a cup of *spiritual* needs. When the cup of
psychological needs is being smashed, one of our remaining shapes
is a cup. This cup is not, however, a cup that says "Jesus, make me
happy," or "Jesus, make me feel better about myself." It is a cup that
simply says, "I need Jesus." "I am a spiritual beggar who cannot
pray, obey, or even have physical life apart from the love of Christ."
"I am dead apart from Christ, and I need his grace every moment."
For these needs, Jesus pours out his love to such an extent that it is
impossible for any one person to contain it.

This brings us to our second point, which is that this beautiful
prayer in Ephesians is for *us*. The "you" Paul is praying about is
clearly "you" plural—"you-all." He is speaking to the body of Christ
in Ephesus. The knowledge he prays for is held "together with all
the saints," and the result of that knowledge is that we "reach unity
in the faith and in the knowledge of the Son of God" (Eph. 4:13). We
mirror Christ most clearly when there is unity among God's people
(Eph. 2:19–22). Such unity is achieved not when we are psychological cups, but when we are God's servants.

Of course, this assumes that *individuals* must know the love of

Christ. But the same individuals must realize that, by themselves, they do not constitute the body of Christ. It takes the entire church to provide a vague imitation of the glory of God. This has been the message throughout Scripture.

According to Ephesians, what do we really need? We need to be a corporate body, smitten with the glory of God, committed to the unity of the church, deluged by his love, and faithful as we walk together in obedience to him, even in our suffering. We need to need other people less and love other people more.

All this takes us full circle. The question was, Who are we? But our answer leaves us looking at Jesus. It can be no other way. An accurate knowledge of ourselves forces us to look to Jesus. After all, we are to be filled with Christ and, like mirrors, reflect his glory. To be true reflections of God's holiness, we must look at Jesus, the true image of God. We are offspring who aspire to be like our Father. So we watch the Father in action. We imitate his holiness.

For Further Thought

This chapter clarifies the biblical perspective on who we are. Its focus has been the image of God in us. Do you have a concise definition yet? To be created in the image of God means that we are like God in every way a creature can be like him, *to the praise of his glorious grace* (Eph. 1:6, 12, 14). This indicates that God has given us gifts to serve rather than needs to be served. Any other perspective is less than biblical and will ultimately lead us toward misery rather than joy.

1. Write thirty applications of the petition, "Hallowed be your name." How can you hallow God's name at work? At rest? With your family? At church?

2. Begin reading some of the prayers in Scripture through the lens of "This is what I need."

3. Consider how this knowledge of God and knowledge of yourself can encourage you to take small steps of obedience in your work and relationships.

CHAPTER

DELIGHT IN THE GOD
WHO FILLS US

"NO man can take a survey of himself but he must immediately turn to the contemplation of God in whom he lives and moves."[1] This is especially true after seeing that many of our needs are more accurately called lusts, and the objects of these needs are called idols. As we grow in self-knowledge, we want to have that knowledge woven together with our knowledge of God. Therefore, having repented where repentance was needed, we should listen again to what God says about himself.

When we listen to God after difficult self-examination, God reveals himself as the Welcoming One. No "I told you so." No time-outs in a spiritual isolation room. Instead, God rejoices that we have turned to him in a more wholehearted way. God promises the repentant person, "None of the offenses he has committed will be remembered against him" (Ezek. 18:22).

If you don't believe that, stop reading immediately. Don't say,

---

1 John Calvin, *Institutes of the Christian Religion,* trans. J. Allen (Philadelphia: Presbyterian Board of Christian Education, 1936), 1.1.1.

"How could God forgive me for *that!*" (whatever *that* is). Don't think that God's forgiveness is a begrudging forgiveness and with that thought deny some of God's glorious love. And don't think that God's promises are only for other people. If this is how you are thinking, you must realize that your own sins, no matter how big, are not bigger than God's pleasure in forgiveness.

This is a time when you must be controlled by the truth of God more than your own feelings. God's Word, not feelings, is our standard. To be driven by our fluctuating sense of well-being may seem spiritual, but it is wrong. It exalts our interpretation above God's. This is why it is so important to immediately turn to God after any biblically guided introspection. When we listen to God, he speaks words that fill an empty soul.

Do you remember the three aspects of the fear of man?

1. We fear people because they can expose and humiliate us.
2. We fear people because they can reject, ridicule, or despise us.
3. We fear people because they can hunt, attack, or threaten us.

God has not forgotten the shamed, rejected, and threatened. We have already discussed how he blesses and frees us by saying, "Fear me and me alone." This is exactly what we need. It gives us the privilege of being controlled by our loving and just Savior rather than other people.

We have also found that our sinful hearts intensify all shame, threat, and rejection, and, again, our God provides the treatment: "Confess that you have been committed to your own desires rather than mine." This gives us the privilege of fearing God because of his immense, forgiving love.

At this point we might think that God has done more than enough, and, indeed, he has. But God's love knows no boundaries: his glory is unending. He knows that we may still experience shame, fear, and rejection in this life. These no longer rule us, but they certainly hurt. It is then that God overwhelms us with even more blessings.

1. To the shamed and humiliated, he covers and glorifies.
2. To the rejected, he accepts and glorifies.
3. To the threatened, he protects and glorifies.

STEP 6 *Rejoice that God has covered your shame, protected you from danger, and accepted you. He has filled you with his love.*

In other words, God fills us. He pours out his love into our hearts by the Holy Spirit, whom he has given us (Rom. 5:5). God actually showers us with himself.

Why didn't we talk about this before? Isn't this news too good to keep in the closet? The reason we are considering this now is that there is a precondition to this blessing. It is not available to us when we adopt the shape of a cup of psychological needs. That is, if we want to be filled so that we can feel happy and better about ourselves, then we will never be truly deluged with God's love. The cup of our own desires is never able to catch the flood of God's love and blessing. Rather, it makes God's redeeming love less accessible to us.

When this cup of "I wants" is broken, it leaves us with a number of shapes or identities that God has given us: priests, ambassadors, children of God, and Christians. Another is that we are empty, humble, needy vessels. We are empty cups. This cup, however, represents our *spiritual* need for forgiveness of sins, covering from shame, protection from oppressors, and acceptance into God's family. It is an emptiness that says, "I need Jesus." It is an emptiness that needs God's love.

So we *do* need the love of Jesus. Since we were created by the

Divine Lover, we will never be okay unless we know deeply of that love. Without this love we are spiritually and physically dead.

This means that lust or selfish desire is not the only explanation for our desire for love. It is typically the most prominent reason, but it does not stand alone. Sometimes the desire for love is the tainted remains of our knowledge of God. When we are lost in sin, without clear spiritual reference points, we misinterpret and distort that knowledge. We think it safer and more effective to look to other people to relieve our emptiness. In some cases, when love is sweet, we might even feel that we have found it. Sadly, this feeling misleads us. It reinforces our sinful idea that people might be the answer to our need, so we pursue them with an obsession. The love that we desire, however, can only be found in the living God.

Hosea's Love Story

One of the great revelations of God's love for us is found in the Old Testament book of Hosea. The book is actually two love stories that run parallel. The real story is about God and his love for his people. The earthly analogy is the story of Hosea and Gomer. Hosea and Gomer point us to God's comfort and pursuing love for the shamed, threatened, and rejected.

The story of Hosea is filled with many questions. Why did God tell Hosea to marry Gomer, a woman who had probably been a prostitute and wasn't planning to stop after she married Hosea? Doesn't God care about marriage? Shouldn't marriage be a committed union?

These questions are exactly the point of the story. None of us could imagine marrying someone like Gomer. There was nothing attractive about her from beginning to end. Yet this was the way that Hosea would get a glimpse into the heart of God, because God *did* marry someone like Gomer.

God was saying to Hosea, in effect, "You and I are both going to give our hearts completely to someone who will utterly reject us. We will give all of our hearts, energy, time, and money in pursuit of them. By doing this, you, Hosea, will understand my faithful love for you and your people. You see, I, myself, am the husband. Your life will be about my love. Your pain will point to my own. And your faithfulness will be a replica of mine."

This was Hosea's ordination to the ministry. Whereas Isaiah was ushered into the throne room and witnessed the majesty and purity of the Holy One, Hosea met Gomer in the seat of sinners and witnessed the unfathomable love of the Holy One. That love was to be Hosea's message to Israel.

> *When the LORD began to speak through Hosea, the LORD said to him, "Go, take to yourself an adulterous wife and children of unfaithfulness, because the land is guilty of the vilest adultery in departing from the LORD." So he married Gomer daughter of Diblaim, and she conceived and bore him a son. (Hos. 1:2–3)*

The pain of rejection and betrayal started quickly for Hosea. At least by the time their second child was born, Gomer was a committed harlot. Gomer's second child was named Lo-Ruhamah, meaning Not Loved. Chances are that this daughter was not even Hosea's. With the third child there is no doubt. His name, Lo-Ammi, means Not My People. By this time, Gomer was coming and going as she pleased.

As we read of this so-called marriage, our minds are jumping from Hosea and his painful plight to God's holy patience and unceasing faithfulness to us. We are beginning to think, *How could God have ever asked me to be his bride?* Undoubtedly, Hosea's mind, too, was jumping from his own situation to a deeper understanding of God's great love.

But Hosea's problems were not over. After disgracing both Hosea and herself, Gomer threw off the appearance of marriage and left Hosea. Deluded by her passions, she somehow thought that she could get something better. She said, "I will go after my lovers, who give me my food and my water, my wool and my linen, my oil and my drink" (Hos. 2:5).

Evidently, when Gomer left, Hosea made sure she had provisions. He knew that her lovers cared nothing for her. They would let her die of starvation, given the chance. So Hosea provided for Gomer, even though she attributed the provisions to her lovers. To Gomer, Hosea was all but forgotten, yet both Hosea and God say, "I was the one who gave her the grain, the new wine and oil, who lavished on her the silver and gold" (Hos. 2:8).

Even with Hosea's support, Gomer was eventually discarded by her lovers. We can only guess the extent of her abuse from these men. Rape, forced prostitution, and beatings were probably the norm for her. She was treated like refuse. All that was left for her was slavery.

Gomer was now done. Her adulteries had led her almost to the grave. She was an outcast, beyond hope. Her shame, fear, and rejection could not have been more intense. She was standing in the slave market, naked so that she could be inspected by potential buyers. Who was going to be the next one to heap abuses on her?

> The LORD said to me [Hosea], "Go, show your love to your wife again, though she is loved by another and is an adulteress. Love her as the LORD loves the Israelites." (Hos. 3:1)

The bidding never went that high. Apparently, nobody was impressed with the merchandise. Gomer was sold for the price of a common slave. After paying the fee, Hosea went over to Gomer and did something that must have left the townspeople whispering to each other: he covered her nakedness. Perhaps Gomer did not even recognize Hosea yet, but that didn't matter. Following God's command, Hosea immediately treated her as his wife. He reaffirmed his covenant of marriage to her. He essentially said, "I am yours and you are mine. I belong to you alone, you belong to me and no other."

Short of the gospel of Christ, this is the greatest love story ever told. Have you ever witnessed this kind of love? I have seen glimpses of it. It exists throughout the church. But nothing truly parallels the story of Hosea and the heavenly story behind it. This is a holy love. Gomer was committed to her own desires. She looked everywhere to be filled. Hosea was committed to being a reflection of the Divine Husband. He knew it was impossible to satisfy his wife's lusts, but he kept wooing her, imploring her to turn away from her own desires and find satisfaction in marital love. Finally, he redeemed her. He bought her back.

What was all this like for Hosea? We don't really know. It had to be a painful life, filled with shame and grief, but Hosea does not offer his personal reflections. What he reports is that he simply submitted to his Lord and obeyed.

What has this been like for our Holy God? In contrast to Hosea, God *has* given us a profound insight into his own heart. It can be found in Hosea 11. But before considering the heart of God for his people, consider how unprecedented it is for anyone to publicly share his or her deepest feelings in the midst of unrequited love. Isn't it humiliating when people know that you are the passionate pursuer who is not even *recognized* by the one being pursued? You feel like a fool. God, however, opens himself to us in one of the most dramatic passages in the Bible.

In the passage that follows, remember that we ourselves are Ephraim; *we* are Israel.

> *How can I give you up, Ephraim?*
> > *How can I hand you over, Israel?*
> *How can I treat you like Adamah?*
> > *How can I make you like Zeboiim?*
> *My heart is changed within me;*
> > *all my compassion is aroused.*
> *I will not carry out my fierce anger,*
> > *nor will I devastate Ephraim again.*
> *For I am God, and not man—*
> > *the Holy One among you.*
> *I will not come in wrath. (Hos. 11:8–9)*

God begins by posing a question, "How can I give you up?" Then he gives an immediate answer, "I cannot! It is impossible. You are mine." God says that he will not treat his rebellious people in the same way he allowed two sister cities of Sodom to be destroyed (Deut. 29:23).

Now notice the word "changed." It is the word God uses to describe his own heart, "My heart is changed within me." This word is rarely used in the Bible as a description of someone's emotional experience. Instead, it is often used to describe the overthrow and destruction of a city. As such, when used to describe emotional experiences, it connotes something *gut-wrenching*. God is saying that his insides are in turmoil on behalf of his people. This is not so much God's talking about the pain of betrayal as it is God's revealing his intense compassion for his people. It reveals the depth of his desire to bring his people back to himself.

Does this surprise you? It does me. I still sometimes get the sense that God let me barely slip in the door of his kingdom. The good folks are already in. I made it because God *had* to let me in. I have professed faith in Jesus as risen Lord and Christ, and therefore, God didn't have a choice.

Yet God did have a choice, and he chose to love us with a passionate, faithful love. The reason I occasionally doubt is that I am thinking that God is like us—or like me. If Gomer were my wife, my instinct would be to let her go and say "Good riddance." I would want to cut my losses and avoid the humiliation of pursuing someone who ignored me. But the passage says that God is not like me. God is God, not a man. "If we are faithless, he will remain faithful, for he cannot disown himself" (2 Tim. 2:13). Moreover, this is not a stoic faithfulness. It is vulnerable and passionate. It is a faithfulness so intense that God describes it as tearing at his insides.

From this you can understand how misguided it is to judge God from the perspective of what we would do in a situation. The temporal and sinful is never the standard for the holy. If we judge by our own experience, we will assume that God will eventually get fed up with us and leave us naked in the slave market. But God says to us, "I am God, and not man—the Holy One among you. I will not come in wrath."

What restrained his wrath, especially considering that God is Holy Love *and* Holy Justice? The reason he did not come in wrath was that his holy justice was anticipating the time when Jesus would become the slave for us. He would take the shame and rejection that was rightfully our own. In its place, he would completely forgive and justify us. Even more, he would glorify us (Rom. 8:30). He would exalt us.

God looks at his creation from the perspective of the consummation. From that vantage point he sees what his Gomer will be. She will be a radiant bride, honored and glorified. She will be presented before God's glorious presence without fault, and she will be received by him with great joy (Jude 24). If God is passionate about pursuing an adulterous wife, you can be certain that there will be great celebration, laughter, and joy when his wife is glorified and in his presence forever.

The scene will be similar to some of the best marriage ceremonies that you have ever witnessed, but since it is a holy wedding, it will be different from those you have seen. One difference will be the focal point of the event. In traditional Western weddings, the bride is the honored one. Everyone at the wedding talks about how beautiful she is. All eyes are consistently on her. At the heavenly, eternal ceremony, however, our gaze will be fixed on another. The bride, indeed, will be exalted, honored, and glorified, but her beauty will exalt the triune God even more. It was he who pursued, wooed, bought, and transformed her. Any beauty in the bride is a reflection of the greater beauty of the bridegroom.

Are you feeling filled yet? This is what God gives to those who have come to know Christ through faith:

➤ The shamed are covered and glorified. They no longer have to hide from the gaze of other people or the gaze of God. They are seen from the perspective of eternity. To them, Jesus says, "Come, come."

➤ The threatened are comforted and glorified. They are comforted because they know that their husband is the sovereign King over all the earth. Will there be suffering? Yes. He will allow refining suffering to come to his bride, but it will be suffering that will lead to good. It will teach his bride to trust in him alone. As a result, blessing will outweigh pain. The blessing of being more like Jesus is greater than the hardship of the refining fire.

➤ The rejected are accepted and glorified. They should stand in awe that God is passionate for them. His acceptance is not begrudging. Instead, it is accompanied by his rejoicing and singing.

Our God no longer calls us slaves. Through Jesus, he calls us friends, children, and his bride. Through his Spirit, he gives us the greatest gift we could ever have. He gives us himself. He says, "I am with you" (cf. John 14:27–28). "'Never will I leave you; never will I forsake you.' So we can say with confidence, 'The Lord is my helper; I will not be afraid. What can man do to me?'" (Heb. 13:5–6).

I knew a man who decided at the moment his wife left him that he would never trust another person again. He would never reveal himself. He would never get close to anyone or let someone else get close to him. Of course, he realized that he was still being controlled by his wife, but he thought this approach at least would be less painful.

In light of Hosea, such a strategy is no longer an option for the Christian. God's love is a costly love. It never takes the easy path away from relationships. Instead, it plots how to move toward other people. It thinks creatively of ways to surprise them with love.

The path of God's love is not without suffering. In fact, those who love more will suffer more. Yet the path of God's love is a path that leaves us overflowing. Our cup cannot contain what God bestows on us. It is only natural, then, that the comfort we received from Christ will overflow into the lives of other people (2 Cor. 1:3–7). Our goal is to love people more than need them. We are overflowing pitchers, not leaky cups.

For Further Thought

Many people ask, "How can I really know God's love? I want to know it, but it seems so distant." The answer is to repent of seeking God so that you can feel better about yourself. Then think about Jesus through the story of Hosea. Ask God to teach you about this love, so you can both know it and give it. Ask other people to pray for you as you read. God promises that he will teach you.

LOVE YOUR ENEMIES AND YOUR NEIGHBORS

THERE is one more step. So far, we have considered the fear of the Lord, and we have considered our own hearts. Now we must understand what God says about other people. Who are they? "What are people for?" asked a friend of mine. What kind of shape do *they* have? How have we defined other people, and how does *God* define other people?

Notice some of the common shapes we give others:

➤ People are gas pumps that fill us.

➤ People are sought-after tickets to acceptance and fame.

➤ People are priests who have the power to make us feel clean and okay.

➤ People are terrorists. We never know when they will strike next.

➤ People are dictators whose every word is law. They are in complete control.

Chapter Eleven

Scott Peck, in his best-selling book, *The Road Less Traveled*, suggests that we can shape other people into host organisms. It is not a pretty picture: people are the intestine, we are the worm.

> "I do not want to live. I cannot live without my husband [wife, girlfriend, boyfriend], I love him [or her] so much." And when I respond, as I frequently do, "You are mistaken; you do not love your husband [wife, girlfriend, boyfriend]." "What do you mean?" is the angry question. "I just told you I can't live without him [or her]." I try to explain. "What you describe is parasitism, not love."[1]

The Bible summarizes these various shapes this way: People are our cherished idols. We worship them, hoping they will take care of us, hoping they will give us what we feel we need. What we really need are *biblical* shapes and identities for other people. Then, instead of needing people to fill our desires, we can love people for the sake of God's glory and fulfill the purpose for which we were created.

For me this last step is the hardest. It is not so hard to understand what the Bible says about people—everyone knows that we are supposed to love them—but it is difficult to apply this knowledge. Loving others makes life less comfortable. It means that I give up my own agenda for a Saturday morning in order to help a neighbor. It means that I get hurt more when someone moves away. It means that people stay at our house when I would prefer to be surrounded with just my immediate family.

Isn't that just like God's Word? Just when we think we have adapted it to a comfortable middle-class lifestyle, it messes every-

---

1   M. Scott Peck, *The Road Less Traveled* (New York: Simon & Schuster, 1978), 98.

thing up. It tells us to love others in the same way that we have been loved by God.

STEP 7   *Need other people less, love other people more. Out of obedience to Christ, and as a response to his love toward you, pursue others in love.*

Enemies

One shape that other people have does not exactly engender love and community, but it is a shape they have nonetheless. People can be enemies. They can be consistently against us. They can plot our destruction and be committed to shaming and disgracing us.

As a counselor I have reminded many Christians that a person is their enemy. Usually people did not want to hear it, but it was true. Even worse, many of these enemies were friends or family.

> *If an enemy were insulting me,*
> *I could endure it;*
> *if a foe were raising himself against me,*
> *I could hide from him.*
> *But it is you, a man like myself,*
> *my companion, my close friend,*
> *with whom I once enjoyed sweet fellowship*
> *as we walked with the throng at the house of God.*
> *(Ps. 55:12–13)*

This passage points most clearly to Jesus' enemy, Judas. But Judas has had many imitators. I remember those who had husband enemies, wife enemies, brother enemies, parent enemies, children enemies, co-worker enemies, and church enemies. The list is too long.

Chapter Eleven

God Responds to Our Enemies

A biblical example of a true enemy is found in the book of Esther. If there was ever a biblical Hitler, it was Haman, egomaniacal and with an insane determination to extinguish all the Hebrew people (Est. 3–5). At first, Haman's jealous rage was directed toward the Jew, Mordecai. Soon, he generalized his hatred to all Israel.

Following the example of Daniel, Mordecai would not bow down to other people. To do so would have dishonored the true God. The problem was that Haman, second only to King Xerxes in authority, was full of himself, yet he wanted to be fuller. He demanded that Mordecai bow down to him, just as everyone else did.

When Mordecai's refusal was reported to Haman, Haman was enraged and immediately committed himself to a plan that would do more than kill Mordecai. "He scorned the idea of killing only Mordecai. Instead Haman looked for a way to destroy all Mordecai's people, the Jews, throughout the whole kingdom of Xerxes" (Est. 3:6).

Here is a true enemy. Even Esther said so. Esther was the zenith of graciousness and gentility, so if Esther said something unbecoming of a person, you knew that such a person was treacherous. "The adversary and enemy is this vile Haman," she said to the king (Est. 7:6).

Most of us have *never* had an enemy like Haman. Our perceived enemies are people who may have slighted us or sinned against us a time or two. To have someone dedicated to our annihilation is indeed rare. Yet there are Hamans in the world. What do we do with them?

First, we should know that God hears the voice of the oppressed. He has compassion on them, and the oppressor arouses his anger. Second, God blesses victims with the knowledge that he is bigger than our enemies. As the book of Proverbs teaches, God will never allow enemies ultimately to triumph.

These men [enemies] lie in wait for their own blood; they waylay only themselves! Such is the end of all who go after ill-gotten gain; it takes away the lives of those who get it. (1:18–19; also 12:7; 16:25; 24:16)

The years of the wicked are cut short. (10:27)

When pride comes, then comes disgrace. (11:2; also 13:21; 16:5, 18; 18:12)

When a wicked man dies, his hope perishes; all he expected from his power comes to nothing. (11:7; also 14:11)

A false witness will not go unpunished, and he who pours out lies will perish. (19:9; also 21:28)

Do not fret because of evil men or be envious of the wicked, for the evil man has no future hope, and the lamp of the wicked will be snuffed out. (24:19–20)

These proverbs aptly describe the story of Haman. Shortly after the king agreed to Haman's request to annihilate the Jews, Haman was disgraced by being forced to show great honor to Mordecai. Soon after that, the gallows that Haman had erected for Mordecai were used on Haman himself. Finally, all of his property was given to Mordecai.

God says that some people are best defined as enemies. When we encounter them, our proper response is first to trust God rather than fear man. We trust that God, not the enemy, is the Almighty. Enemies, after all, will not last.

> *Do not put your trust in princes,*
> *in mortal men, who cannot save.*
> *When their spirit departs, they return to the ground;*
> *on that very day their plans come to nothing. (Ps. 146:3–4)*

> *Do not fear the reproach of men or be terrified by their insults.*
> *For the moth will eat them up like a garment; and the worm*
> *will devour them like wool. (Isa. 51:7–8)*

This does not mean that we can smugly think, "You'll get yours." Not at all. The Scripture makes it clear that we should never gloat when our enemy falls (Prov. 24:17). It simply means that enemies will die. They are flesh that will fade away. In other words, they are like us! But that is not all. The biblical teaching about enemies also indicates that their legacy of evil will end. The kingdom of heaven will overpower it. It will not last.

Such a promise might not mean exactly what we think, however. If we interpret it through the lens of our personal desires, it means that we personally will be vindicated. We would actually witness the overthrow of our enemy. But the promise doesn't mean that. Some enemies have been known to last for generations. What it means is that enemies will not restrain the growth of God's kingdom, the church. For example, Assyria could not thwart God's plan. Today Assyria does not exist, but the church of God has spread throughout the world (cf. Ps. 126).

This promise is exciting only if we think corporately more than individually. Isaiah did not live to see the demise of Assyria, but the prophecy against it was a great comfort to him. He knew that he would not see the end of Assyrian rule, but he could rejoice that God's people would flourish and God would be exalted.

The Comfort of Jesus in the Psalms

When confronted with enemies, we should go directly to the Psalms if we are not sure how to feel or what to say. In them, we are given exactly what we need. What the Psalms do is lean against some of our natural instincts. When we are inclined to take matters into our own hands, the Psalms teach us to trust God. When we would insulate ourselves from pain, they teach us to trust God. Instead of vowing that we will never again move close to another person, we learn to trust God. Instead of extinguishing hope, the Psalms teach us to trust God and, as a result, be filled with jubilant expectations for the coming of the kingdom. You could say that the Psalms improve our quality of life.

The Psalms are often so precise in articulating our sufferings that we think they were written just for us. And that is true—they *were* written for us, but they also serve another purpose. When psalmists like King David described their suffering at the hands of their enemies, they intended to write something more than auto-biographical statements that future generations could use to com-miserate with them. The Psalms were worthy of inclusion into Scripture because David was a representative of the Divine King. He asked for judgment against his enemies because they were enemies of the true God. It was the glory of God that was David's mission, not his own vindication.

To be more specific, King David spoke on behalf of the greater king, King Jesus. The enemies of which he spoke are those of Jesus; the sufferings of which he spoke are those of the Messiah. This means that we should read each psalm at least twice. The first time we can allow it to speak for us. The second time we listen to it as the voice of Jesus. Once again, this will encourage us in the fear of the Lord. We will find that Jesus' pain was greater than our own. As P. J. Forsyth rightly said, "What happens to the sinful creatures of God, however tragic, is less monstrous than what happened to the Son of God."

This doesn't minimize the pain of persecution and threats, but it does draw our attention outward—away from both ourselves and our enemies. It means that when we are confronted by an enemy, our prayers can transcend our personal turmoil. Certainly, we should pray for deliverance, but the Psalms provoke us to pray even bigger prayers. Even in the midst of Haman-like threats, the Psalms teach us to pray that the name of Jesus would be exalted. We will pray that God's kingdom would advance and overwhelm all enemies of the light, especially Satan himself.

If Your Enemy Is Hungry, Feed Him

One reason it is critical to look toward Jesus when faced with our enemies is that it makes God's next words less shocking. God may define some people as enemies, but he says that we are to treat them as friends. Our duty is to consider how to serve them in such a way that they would be pointed to Jesus and repent from their sins.

Now you can understand why this last step of knowing other people (and acting on that knowledge) is so difficult. How can we even begin this impossible process? According to God's Word, it begins with the knowledge that we have been disobedient. We have violated God's prohibitions and failed to love as we ought. Do we realize that we were Christ's enemies? If we do, then we have no choice but to treat enemies the way God has treated us. Our conscience would rebel if we felt smug in a self-righteous judgment of our enemies.

What about the phrase, "In doing this, you will heap burning coals on his head" (Rom. 12:20)? This hint of revenge might make the task of loving enemies a little easier. But be careful on this one. There is no biblical command that is ever tainted by thoughts of revenge. I know some men and women who seemed quite pious toward their enemies, but their hearts missed the intent of Scripture. They thought, "Great, I have a way to get back at my father without having to go to jail. I will be sickening sweet to him, and it will drive him crazy." Yet the intent of the passage is a holy intent. The purpose of the burning coals is to bring the offender to repentance and faith. For many people, that is beyond the scope of their love. The idea of showing temporary, earthly mercy to the offender is one thing, but the thought that the offender could be forgiven and accepted as a child of God is sometimes too much. If it is too much, we must pray that we would not be overcome by evil. Instead, we must pray that we would have Jesus' love for the offender. We must invite others to pray with and for us too.

Love Your Enemies

Feeding enemies is an application of the larger principle of loving your enemies. God says that you treat enemies the same way you treat friends and family. Impossible? Of course. But not when we have the fear of the Lord. When we know that God's power is greater than that of our enemies, when we know that he is just, and when we know that he loved us while we were his enemies, then we are free to be simple servants who imitate and obey the Father. He blesses the righteous and unrighteous with rain and food, and so we too should bless (Matt. 5:45).

To love in this way, we need both power and discernment. We need power because we are incapable of loving the way Christ has loved us. We need discernment because it is sometimes difficult to know what form love should take. As a result, anytime we are aware that we have specific enemies, we should seek counsel from the church in order to discern how to express that love. Too often, people interpret the command to love our enemies as "give them whatever they want from you." There are times when such expressions of love are unwise.

Should a woman divorced by her husband give him what he wants in a divorce settlement? Shouldn't she treat her husband the way she would want to be treated? Common sense says, "No, don't give the rat anything." But is this—minus the "rat"—a biblical way to proceed? Perhaps so. Love, in this case, will mean to forgive her enemy, not slander him to others, and not attack him with words in order to get some measure of revenge. But love is not the only category that applies to this situation. There is also justice. If her husband is threatening and asking for things that are simply unfair, the woman should plead for justice and the church should plead with her.

Love for enemies is the pinnacle of Christian obedience to God. As the Sermon on the Mount indicates, it is easy to love people who love you. But it demands a powerful work of God's Spirit to love those who are committed to harming you.

There is one other thing you should know about loving your enemies. In light of the book of Hosea, this should not be a surprise. On the surface, love for enemies sounds like self-punishment or foolishness. It goes in the face of popular counsel that tells you to jettison people who damage your self-esteem. But if God says it, it must be good. There is always a blessing in obedience. The blessing might not be reconciliation or repentance by the enemy. Instead, it may be the privilege of not being controlled by that enemy. Or it might simply be the joy of becoming more like Jesus. Whatever it may be, there is always a blessing in obedience.

Neighbors and Foreigners

A second group of people are those who are not part of the visible church. In the Old Testament such people were called foreigners or aliens; in the New Testament they are called neighbors.

A Love Based on Kinship

Old Testament Israel had very clear laws protecting foreigners living in the land. Solomon, in an inspired prayer, prayed that God would answer all the prayers of foreigners, "so that all the peoples of the earth may know your name and fear you" (1 Kings 8:43). Aliens were not to be mistreated (Ex. 22:21) or deprived justice (Mal. 3:5); instead, they were to be given land (Ezek. 47:22) and loved (Deut. 10:19). The book of Ruth is about an alien—a Moabitess—who was included in the royal line of David and Jesus.

All this was an imitation of God's love to Israel, who themselves had been aliens (Ex. 22:21; 23:9; Lev. 19:34). In fact, they were always aliens. "The land is mine," said the Lord, "and you are but aliens and my tenants" (Lev. 25:23). As aliens who were blessed by God, they were to treat other people the way God had treated them.

The New Testament is replete with the command to love God and neighbor (Matt. 22:39; James 2:8). The classic amplification of this command is Jesus' story of the Good Samaritan (Luke 10:25–37). In this story, Jesus expands the normal boundaries of neighbors to the point where the story is about two enemies, a Jew and a Samaritan. Then, Jesus makes the hero of the story the Samaritan, whom the Jews considered to be their moral inferior. He could not have made his point any more powerfully.

This is very relevant to some of my past family discussions. My wife and I have two daughters. When they were younger, they were

The Loud Children when they were with us, but they seemed to be deaf and dumb with neighbors or people they didn't know well.

You can imagine their explanation when we pointed this out. "Shy," they said. "Rude," we'd retort.

It may be true that some children are naturally more timid around people, but a great deal of shyness is the child's version of the fear of other people. They are being controlled by others.

The best treatment was for Sheri and me to discuss with our children some applications of Jesus' command to love our neighbor. We talked about how Jesus has welcomed us, then we considered how to "do to others what you would have them do to you" (Matt. 7:12). We joked with them about the sudden affliction they developed around new people, and we would role-play some alternatives with them. We suggested to them that one word answers, or grunts, were illegal.

Progress was slow. Our children are just like us: they learn through incessant repetition, practice, and prayer. Sanctification is like a clumsy, slow walk rather than a light switch that we turn from off to on. But by God's grace we grow. My children are rarely zombie-like when they meet new people now. When we prepare them and pray for them, they change.

Of course, if they wanted to turn the tables on us, they could just say, "Evangelism." The fear of man is no respecter of persons. It might be called codependency with adults, peer pressure with teens, and shyness with children, but whatever it is called, it all betrays the same idolatrous heart. To avoid this snare I need my children to pray and to exhort me in the same way they need Sheri and me to pray for them.

The prescription for timid evangelists is now in place. Once we understand the depth of the problem we can begin by seeking the fear of the Lord. It is much easier to talk about Jesus when his life consistently leaves us in awe. Then we repent of our fear of other people's rejection. Isn't that a prominent reason for our timidity? We worship the acceptance and favor of all people. When we sense the least bit of rejection, we crumble. Finally, we remember what God says about other people: we are to need them less and love them more. I don't need them to fill up my love cup; instead, I am in their debt. I owe them a debt of love which can be paid, in small part, by pointing them to the love of Jesus.

For Further Thought

The command to love enemies and neighbors is an unavoidable implication of knowing God and knowing ourselves. If we have been God's enemies, and God has come close to us and reconciled us to himself, what can we do except treat others as we have been treated? As we imitate Jesus in this way we will be salt and light in our generation.

1. Pick one enemy and one neighbor and begin to pray for them.

2. Look for opportunities to surprise someone outside the body of Christ with love.

CHAPTER

LOVE YOUR BROTHERS AND SISTERS

EVERYONE, Jesus indicated, is our neighbor, and we are to show grace and mercy to everyone because God has been gracious and merciful to us. Yet those within the body of Christ are our family in a unique way. They are the ones with whom we will spend eternity, and they are the ones whose partnership we need in order to represent Christ.

The apostle Paul said, "As we have opportunity, let us do good to all people, *especially* to those who belong to the family of believers" (Gal. 6:10). This certainly does not diminish our concern for neighbors and enemies; rather, such special concern is a natural result of being family in the most intimate sense of the word.

This kind of love and unity does not come without a battle. The same adversaries that oppose the fear of the Lord—the world, the flesh, and the Devil—also oppose the exhortation to love and be united with other brothers and sisters. It would be wise to keep one eye on these enemies as we talk about the church as family.

Remember, (1) the flesh has a sinful bent toward self-interest. It is committed to the question, "What's in it for me?" (2) Satan is a liar and divider. Notice that the most explicit biblical teaching on spiritual warfare (Eph. 6) is found in the book that emphasizes unity. Satan's most prominent strategy is to fracture and divide. And (3) the world tries to institutionalize these tendencies.

Let me bring these dark opponents more into the open.

"I want you to forget about institutions," said the evangelist. "The gospel is not about churches. It is about a decision you make before Jesus and nobody else."

What do you think of his approach? He is right that individual people must "repent and be baptized" (Acts 2:38). And I can understand that some people have a warped view of the church, so the evangelist did not want those preconceptions to cloud the spiritual issues. But isn't the call to trust and obey a broader call than "Jesus and me"? The promises of God are "for you and your children and for all who are far off—for all whom the Lord our God will call" (Acts 2:39). And isn't the person being called to Christ, who is the head of an institution? When people were converted in the book of Acts, it was assumed that they would be part of a local fellowship. It could have been no other way. They had been ushered into a *community* of the resurrection, a community of the Spirit.

Recently there was an interesting study that contrasted the Japanese response to personal trials with the American response. The question was, How did people comfort themselves during these difficulties? The Japanese consistently said, "I think about my family. I imagine that my family is with me." The American response was typically, "I can overcome this, I just have to work harder." Or there was self-talk that was intended to inflate the needy self: "I'm great. This person can't beat me. I am better than he is." In other words, we live in a culture that emphasizes the individual over the corporate.

Americans often use variations on the phrase "self-reliance."

This phrase is a notorious problem for translators. For example, in Latin America, the closest they can come is a word more like our "independence" in that it is political and social, not personal. In some Asian countries the phrase makes no sense, or it is a sign of mental instability. The person should never be self-reliant, according to most Asian traditions. The person should be interdependent.

I once heard a Christian variation of Frank Sinatra's "I Did It My Way." It was called, "I Did It His Way." Please don't think I am picking at nits here. I simply want to keep my eyes open to the insidious ways we think privately rather than corporately. Do you see my concern with this retitled song? Certainly "his" is better than "my," but wouldn't "we" be more accurate than "I"? The song retains its isolated feel. It is "Jesus and me."

Do you remember the Christian woman who said that God told her to marry someone who was not a Christian? That may have been an extreme example, but how often do we consult with pastors, elders, and those in our church when we are thinking about marriage, a job change, or other major decisions? How often do I ask for prayer from the body when I am writing or speaking? There is always a lot of discussion and instruction about knowing God's personal will for our lives, but do you ever hear people talking about God's will for the church or even for their family?

Have you ever noticed that for many people, church as family doesn't exist? More often I overhear people who talk as if the church were their enemy. Sometimes these people have been hurt by people in the church and then make a decision not to be hurt again. They generalize from the specific case to the entire church: If one person hurt me, then the church hurt me. At other times, we act as if the church is an enemy because of our own sense of shame. In other words, since we can see the things in our lives that shame us, we assume that others see them too. Usually, however, we treat the church as an enemy because we have not been taught by the Scriptures. We don't know what God says about his body.

This has everything to do with the fear of man. When we think of ourselves as alone and isolated, we will always be prone to fear other people. Isolation and the fear of man are close companions. Yet when we truly understand that God has called us to participate in a larger family (i.e., the church), we are free. Church begins to feel a little more like a family sitting with us in our living room. Better yet, we feel like a family sitting together at the feet of Jesus, sitting around the throne. With family, there is no self-consciousness, no embarrassment, no fear.

You may not have come from a solid family. Your home may have been a place where you were always being criticized and always wondering what others might be thinking. If so, don't let your experience of family corrupt your understanding of what God says about it. You must believe that those in the body of Christ are your family. Learn that we are a *people* just as much as we are individual *persons*. This lesson is not necessarily easier for people who have come from good families. This is because the lesson is learned by faith, not simply by previous experience.

Notice the results if we neglect to see the importance of biblical community. If we privatize Scripture, turning "we" into "I," we have the following dilemmas:

➤ I have to go into all the world and make disciples (Matt. 28:18).

➤ I have to pray without ceasing (1 Thess. 5:17).

➤ I have to give proper recognition to the widows who are in need (1 Tim. 5:3).

➤ I have to teach the older men, younger men, and younger women (Titus 2:1–8).

And somehow, in the gaps of my day, I have to work and make enough money for my family.

Fortunately, these commands are given to the church. It is only on the corporate level that we are able to evangelize the world. It takes financial supporters, mission boards, friends and churches that faithfully pray, and many other people in the body for a missionary to go and make disciples. And to fulfill the command to pray without ceasing, I need the church because I need to sleep every now and then, and I have to go to work. Round-the-clock praying can only be done by the worldwide church.

The Corporate Image of God

The foundation for God's teaching on oneness, love, and family goes back to the image of God in man. To image God means to imitate and represent God for the sake of his glory. It means that we are to be like God in every way that creatures can be like the Creator. To remotely imitate such immense glory certainly demands a large group of people, because creatures are limited while God's glory is unlimited. Chapter 9 summarized some of the facets of this glory, and thus portrayed some ways that we can imitate God, but there was one way that was neglected.

Hear, O Israel: The LORD our God, the LORD is one. (Deut. 6:4)

If there were a panoply of gods, divisions and factions would be understandable among religious people. "I am of Zeus." "I am of Mercury." But our God is one, and his people imitate him and bring him glory when they are one.

What was the most prominent identity of the Israelite? "I am an Israelite, the people who belong to God." Try to find "God and me" in the five books of Moses. You will not find it. God's covenant was with a *people*. "Hear, O *Israel*," said the Lord.

> *Walk about Zion, go around her,*
> *count her towers,*
> *consider well her ramparts,*
> *view her citadels,*
> *that you may tell of them to the next generation.*
> *For this God is our God for ever and ever;*
> *he will be our guide even to the end. (Ps. 48:12–13)*

The Old Testament Israelites had *corporate* festivals, the Passover was celebrated with *families,* and there was a yearly day of atonement for the sins of the people as a whole (Lev. 16). Israelites were commanded to talk about God and his law to their children and each other (Deut. 6). The promises were promises to a people just as much as to an individual. Likewise, the curses for individual disobedience were often curses on all the people.

When Achan sinned by taking plunder from Jericho, "*Israel* acted unfaithfully" (Josh. 7:1). The Lord said that Israel had sinned. The punishment for disobedience fell on all the people when the army was routed by the men of Ai. To deal with the sin, all Israel was to be consecrated before the Lord. Of course, the Bible is clear that each individual is responsible for his or her own sin, but there is a sense in which the whole body is polluted when there is sin in one of the members.

Daniel was keenly aware that even in exile, he was joined inextricably with God's people. What was said about them could be said about him. He was shamed by the exile, and he felt the burden of the people's sin.

*O Lord, the great and awesome God, who keeps his covenant
of love with all who love him and obey his commands, we
have sinned and done wrong. We have been wicked and
have rebelled; we have turned away from your commands and
laws. We have not listened to your servants the prophets....
O LORD, we and our kings, our princes and our fathers are
covered with shame because we have sinned against you.
(Dan. 9:4–8)*

I remember an assignment in fourth grade where we had to
write a letter without using "I." I am still not sure what the purpose
was—sometimes I think that since we were such a bad class the
teacher used it to point out our selfishness—but I know that we all
thought it was almost impossible.

The equivalent Christian assignment would be to pray without
praying for specific personal concerns. For me, such praying is as
difficult as writing a letter without "I." When I pray, I typically have
concentric circles in mind. The inner circle is my family, the next
circle my relatives, the next my church, the next missions, and so
on. Too often, I fatigue before I get out of the second circle.

How have you tried to pray "bigger"? It is an excellent remedy
for the fear of man. Try to pray backwards from the outer circle to
the inner, by praying for the world and the church at large before
getting closer to home. Pray prayers from the Bible. Pray the Psalms.
The Psalms are for private meditation *and* for the assembly, but they
are most comfortable in the assembly.

Psalm 133 is an example of an explicitly corporate psalm. It is a
picture of blessings that cannot be contained—descending, descending, and descending. Such a picture is reserved for one of the
greatest blessing that God can give his people—the blessing of
unity.

How good and pleasant it is
when brothers live together in unity!
It is like precious oil poured on the head,
running down on the beard,
running down on Aaron's beard,
down upon the collar of his robes.
It is as if the dew of Hermon
were falling on Mount Zion.
For there the LORD bestows his blessing,
even life forevermore.

The first picture is of Aaron's ordination as a priest. It was a grand day, a day of great celebration. It confirmed God's covenant with his people. God was saying by way of this ordination that he would dwell with his people, and the people would have access to their God through the priests. Then, as we witness the ordination, the oil, which only had to be applied to the head, kept flowing until it covered Aaron. The oil of consecration could not be contained. It just kept descending and descending.

In a similar way, Hermon was the largest mountain in the region, and Zion was not much more than a hill. If the dew of Hermon fell on Zion, it would be a deluge of fruitful blessing in an arid area.

This psalm is a critical prayer for the people of God. When we fear other people and either isolate or protect ourselves from them, we isolate and protect ourselves from a significant part of God's remedy—love and unity with his people. A psalm such as Psalm 133 reminds us to pray for God's remedy. It reminds us that one of the great blessings on earth is to be united with God's people rather than to fear them or be isolated from them.

Unity and Love—A Biblical Priority

Such Old Testament pictures were most likely in the apostle Paul's mind when he wrote to the churches. For example, in his letter to the Ephesians you can almost hear him saying, "How good and pleasant it is when brothers live together in unity."

Yet Paul had much more in mind than unity among those who were Hebrews by birth. He was talking about a unity that the prophets themselves rarely imagined. He envisioned the church: Jew and Gentile, sworn enemies, clean and unclean. It was in this unity that "through the church, the manifold wisdom of God should be *made known to the rulers and authorities in the heavenly realms*" (Eph. 3:10). In other words, Paul's vision of the church is that it would be God's grandest statement to both the world *and* the heavenly beings. The church is being watched and studied by spiritual powers, and it is through the church corporate that the great riches of God's wisdom are being announced. What is the pinnacle of this wisdom? That God has demonstrated his glory by bringing a motley group to himself and uniting them in Christ.

To bring us to unity, God has given gifts to the body. The gifts are other people. Through people—apostles, prophets, evangelists, pastors, teachers, and a host of others—God builds up the church "until we all reach unity in the faith and in the knowledge of the Son of God" (Eph. 4:13).

In other words, to glorify God we need people. We need to be taught and pastored, and we need to teach and pastor. We need daily counsel from our brothers and sisters, and they need counsel from us. We need people to ask us the tough questions, even though there are times when we wish they would let us alone. Even the apostle Paul needed these things: "I long to see you . . . that you and I may be mutually encouraged by each other's faith" (Rom. 1:11–12).

Chuck Swindoll is representative of many people in the church who know they can't grow in grace isolated from other believers. He realizes that the perceived safety of self-protection and lack of vulnerability is actually a curse from which God desires to liberate us. When he was with his fellow pastors, they challenged each other with these seven questions:

1. Have you been with a woman anywhere this past week that might be seen as compromising?
2. Have any of your financial dealings lacked integrity?
3. Have you exposed yourself to any sexually explicit material?
4. Have you spent adequate time in Bible study and prayer?
5. Have you given priority time to your family?
6. Have you fulfilled the mandates of your calling?
7. Have you just lied to me?

To these questions I would add at least one statement. "Now that I have asked you these questions, let me tell you how you have been a blessing to me. Let me tell you how you have pointed me to Christ."

As a counselor, I have spoken with many people who want to know their spiritual gifts. They come hoping for some sort of diagnostic test that will precisely locate them. My impression is that this perspective represents a breakdown in the church. It reflects a church where we are running around as self-actualizing individuals rather than uniting as a God-glorifying community.

For example, persons searching for their gifts think that they can "find" their gifts in isolation from the body. They have forgotten that the orientation of God's people is outward rather than inward. The question should be this: How can I grow in love for and service to the body of Christ? Gifts are the way we naturally love and serve. To paraphrase Augustine, if you want to know your God-given gifts, first know that the purpose of spiritual gifts is to bring unity to the church. Then "love God and do what you feel like doing."

But there is more to the unleashing of gifts in the body. One of the bad fruits of an "I" church is that we don't tell people when they bless us. If someone has taught Sunday school and helped us understand a passage of Scripture, then we should tell the person and encourage his or her gift. If worship leaders left us rejoicing that we have been with God's people in his presence, then thank them for the specific ways they blessed you and the church. No one should have to ask what their gifts are; we should tell people their gifts as they minister to us.

Can you sense the natural outward direction of God's remedy for the fear of man? Although it includes biblically guided self-reflection, the purpose of this introspection is love. God's Word consistently urges us toward love for God and love for other people. As we follow this path, we find that we are no longer dominated by an idolatrous fear of others.

Yet the path is not always easy. In fact, it is rarely easy. Before Jesus returns, we should be prepared for some major bumps—bumps like the ones the apostle Paul found in the Corinthian church.

I appeal to you, brothers, in the name of our Lord Jesus Christ, that all of you agree with one another so that there may be no divisions among you and that you may be perfectly united in mind and thought. (1 Cor. 1:10)

You are still worldly. For since there is jealousy and quarreling among you, are you not worldly? . . . One says, "I follow Paul," and another, "I follow Apollos." (1 Cor. 3:3–4)

The very fact that you have lawsuits among you means you have been completely defeated already. (1 Cor. 6:7)

These divisions were even apparent during the celebration of the Lord's Supper. It wasn't so much that there were fist-fights breaking out before communion (at least Paul does not *report* fist-fights). Paul's stated concern was the chaos that resulted from people acting as isolated, selfish individuals rather than as one body. The recurring theme from the book of Judges fit well: "Everyone did as he saw fit" (Judg. 17:6). With all due respect to teenagers, it was like eating dinner, family style, with a bunch of ravenous, selfish teenage boys. Because of these divisions, the apostle Paul gave specific directions about the Lord's Supper. The apostle told us that we must examine ourselves before participating in the communion table (1 Cor. 11:28).

When you are told to examine yourself before the Lord's Supper, what do you think about? Most likely you remember a list of recent private sins. If you do, great! For some people it is the only quiet moment in their lives, and it is an excellent time for the confession of sin and repentance. Yet, as good as that is, the passage is saying something more. What Paul is exhorting us to examine is our "recognizing the body of the Lord." Are we realizing that the church is one? Are we aware that those with whom we share the Supper are the body of Christ? Our family? This is clearly the context of the passage.

This means that we should remember that it is through Christ's death that we are reconciled to God *and* each other. He has made us one, and we set our hearts on pursuing unity in love. The Lord's Supper is a great time to pray and plan for oneness with our brothers and sisters. It is a time to explore new ways to be kind, compassionate, and forgiving.

The apostle's exhortation also means that we should repent of sins that have divided God's people. Have we gossiped against or slandered anyone? Have we avoided people? Have we been sinfully angry with anyone?

Jesus himself gave specific directions for pursuing this unity.

If you are offering your gift at the altar and there remember that your brother has something against you, leave your gift there in front of the altar. First go and be reconciled with your brother; then come and offer your gift. (Matt. 5:23–24)

When you stand praying, if you hold anything against anyone, forgive him, so that your Father in heaven may forgive you your sins. (Mark 11:25)

The apostle Paul said the same thing in his letter to the Ephesians.

We are all members of one body. "In your anger do not sin": Do not let the sun go down while you are still angry. (Eph. 4:25–26)

Can you sense the urgency in these directions? Only a church that is united in love can truly display God's glory to both spiritual powers and the world, and only a church united can stand against Satan's efforts to divide. The Bible is unequivocal: if you have contributed to a lack of unity, deal with it now. Revivals should start at the Lord's Supper.

One implication of this unity is that it guarantees that the life of a Christian will be filled with greater joy—but also greater sorrow. It will be filled with great joy because Christ has risen, we have been given a community, and, as the Spirit unites us, we rejoice with other brothers and sisters who rejoice. But the life of a Christian is filled with greater sorrow because we suffer when other parts of the body suffer. In the same way that we are affected when one of our family members is suffering, so we are to suffer when those in our extended family are suffering. Also, when we are hurt by people in the body, it will hurt more because they are our family. Such a wound, however, will not be paralyzing. Instead, by God's grace we will grow in faith through it and be ready with the question, What is my duty to this brother or sister?

Our duty, of course, is love. One advantage for us that comes out of the Corinthian divisiveness is that Paul could not end his exhortation about oneness with "Love God and do what you feel" or even "Love one another." Instead, he had to be very specific about what love looked like. He had to define love. As a result, we have been blessed with 1 Corinthians 13.

Jesus' Prayer for Our Unity

If the love and unity of 1 Corinthians 13 sounds impossible, take heart. Even though the world, the flesh, and the Devil are formidable adversaries, Jesus has prayed for us. In doing this, he reminds us of what we need, he gives us a pattern for prayer, and he gives us confidence that since love and unity are God's will, he will bring them into being.

Jesus' prayer in John 17 has already helped us understand some of what we need. We need to bring glory to God, and we need to grow in our sanctification or obedience to the Father. The other theme that is integral to Jesus' prayer is oneness.

Holy Father, protect them by the power of your name—the name you gave me—so that they may be one as we are one. (v. 11)

I pray also for those who will believe in me through their message, that all of them may be one. (vv. 20–21)

May they be brought to complete unity to let the world know that you sent me. (v. 23)

I have made you known to them, and will continue to make you known in order that the love you have for me may be in them and that I myself may be in them. (v. 26)

This is a profound way to bring glory to God. As Jesus and the Father are one, so we are to be one with each other. This is both wonderful and frightening. On one hand, the goal of true biblical community is a great blessing. We have part of God's remedy to the fear of man, and we have access to something the world is begging for. But it means that we must move toward others in love. This is where it can get frightening. People, after all, make our lives messy. Everything is much neater when we can maintain our safe little worlds and be content with being nice and giving money. Now, knowing the teaching of Scripture, such indifference or self-centeredness is impossible.

Unity and love mean:

➤ We confess our sins to each other (James 5:16).

➤ We share with brothers and sisters who are in need (Rom. 12:13; 1 John 3:17).

➤ We are vulnerable with others (Hosea).

➤ We associate with people of low position (Rom. 12:16).

➤ We creatively consider ways to honor others (Rom. 12:10).

➤ We discern when to confront sin and when to overlook it (Matt 18:15; Prov. 17:9; 19:11).

➤ We are patient with everyone (1 Cor. 13:4).

➤ We are willing to sacrifice (John 15:12–13).

➤ We practice church discipline (Matt. 18:15–19; 1 Cor. 5:1–5).

Biblical love is *never* satisfied unless it is growing (1 Peter 1:22). It develops strategies, it asks for prayer from others in order to grow, it thinks big—not big in terms of spectacular but big in terms of something beyond human expectations. Biblical love is not a showy love that draws attention to itself, but it should have grandiose intentions. We *want* it to be witnessed by every living creature. We want all people and all spiritual authorities and powers to know that we are disciples of the living God by our love (John 13:35).

You (Plural) Are God's Tabernacle

All this means that you have yet another identity. You are God's tabernacle, his temple. In the Old Testament, the tabernacle was God's earthly home, his very presence with his people. This is the same tabernacle that left enemy armies in awe. For example, soon after the Philistines captured the ark they quickly removed it from their land: their idol Dagon kept falling down before it. This is the tabernacle that was so holy that when the men of Beth Semesh looked into it, the Lord put them to death. The remaining men of Beth Semesh said, "Who can stand in the presence of the LORD, this holy God?" (1 Sam. 6:20). Likewise, Uzzah was struck down when he tried to brace the teetering ark of God (2 Sam. 6:6–7).

Now shift to the New Testament. "Don't you know that you yourselves are God's temple, and that God's Spirit lives in you"? (1 Cor. 3:16). The apostle Paul is saying that *we* are the tabernacle of God. The church is the tabernacle. Here is one of the mysteries that resided in the Old Testament and was revealed in the New. We, together, have the living God within us. This is the mystery that was glorious and rich, "Christ in you, the hope of glory" (Col. 1:27). It is enough to leave us trembling.

Enemies, Neighbors, and the Body of Christ: In Their Debt

Who are other people? They take on three different shapes: enemies, neighbors, and family. What is our duty to them? Love. Love may take a different form with each group, but our duty is summed up as love. We love enemies by surprising them with our service toward them. We love neighbors by treating them like our family. And we love the body of Christ—our true brothers and sisters—in such a way that the world and spiritual powers are stunned by our oneness.

To put our duty more strongly, we are in *debt* to our enemies, neighbors, and friends. No matter what they have done, and no matter how lopsided our giving to them is in contrast with theirs to us, we are in their debt.

> *Let no debt remain outstanding, except the continuing debt to love one another, for he who loves his fellow man has fulfilled the law. The commandments . . . are summed up in this one rule: "Love your neighbor as yourself." (Rom. 13:8–9)*

Will this love set us up to be hurt? Without question. C. S. Lewis indicated that if he wanted something easy and pain-free, he would have chosen a bottle of wine over Jesus. There is no question that biblical love leaves us more vulnerable. But this will not be the devastating vulnerability that comes with psychologically *needing* people. Christians need less and love more.

Will this debt of love set us up to be manipulated by those who want to use us for their ungodly purposes? Probably not, at least not for long.

A middle-aged pastor was gently rebuked by his physician for doing too much. The physician said that the pastor needed a vacation or he was headed for illness. The pastor, of course, had no time just then for a vacation. He was too busy taking care of his congregation and the special needs of his wife and two daughters.

His wife had been plagued with a mysterious illness over the previous five years to the point where she would no longer drive or go out by herself. This meant that the pastor took her everywhere. Shopping and medical appointments alone accounted for over an hour each day.

The pastor was also teaching two courses at a local seminary because he needed extra money. His one daughter had recently bought a car, and he was paying the insurance. His other daughter was in college, and he was paying all the fees. Neither, however, worked.

With all these things happening, how could the pastor take a break from his duties? He was needed by the congregation and his family.

Or did he need to be needed? The pastor understood the fear of the Lord, but he had not understood himself. He had never considered that his self-sacrifice was serving him more than his family. As a result, he was blinded to other, better ways of loving.

He began to see that "nice" was not the same as love. "Nice" was being perceived as the attentive, sacrificial husband and father. "Nice" was being the opposite of his own father, who was disinterested and distant. But "nice" was killing his family because he could be manipulated into anything.

Gradually, the pastor began to see the veiled selfishness in his actions. He recognized that love was much more than saying "Yes." He asked forgiveness of his wife and children and asked them to pray for him because he wanted to grow to love them deeply. As you might expect, the family was a little confused by what was happening, but the pastor had approached them for forgiveness many times before. This episode wasn't *that* different.

But it was. With the counsel of some close, wise friends, the pastor began to think more clearly about ways to love his family. After a few weeks he sat down with the family and presented his plan.

He told one daughter that he would stop paying her insurance in three months. He told his daughter in college that he would only be able to pay a percentage of her next year's tuition. This gave the family nine months to work together on alternative financing such as jobs or loans. After consulting with his wife's physician, he told his wife that he would no longer drive her to medical appointments. The doctor was thrilled with his decision. The pastor also told his family that he was going to ask for a one-year leave of absence from his seminary duties. This would begin after his next semester of teaching.

Then the real test came. His family didn't think he was being nice! They were angry at him. They said he didn't care. In saying these things they were unknowingly baiting him with his favorite idol. He listened to what the family said and considered it prayerfully and with counsel. But he decided that his decisions were wise and that he would stick with them.

After a few rocky months, the family began to thrive. His daughters decided to get jobs, and they even enjoyed them. His wife became less timid and many of her symptoms improved dramatically. The pastor expressed to the church that he had been wrong to take on so many of the tasks around the church because it limited the gifts of others. He confessed this to the congregation, and the congregation responded by being willing to exert their gifts in serving each other.

People-pleasers can mistake "niceness" for love. When they do, they will be prone to being manipulated by others, and burn-out is sure to follow. People-pleasers can also mistake "yes" for love. But "yes" might be very unwise. It might not be the best way to repay our debt of love. Saying "yes" to one task might keep us from another that is more important. It might mean that we will do something that someone else could have done better. It might mean that we will entrench the sin patterns of other people. It might mean that we interpret the church egocentrically rather than as a body, thinking, "If I don't do it, nobody will."

Therefore, "yes," "being nice," and "self-sacrifice" are not necessarily the same as love. They can be ways that we establish our own personal meaning and identity more than creative expressions of loving others. With these cautions about imitators of love in mind, I want to put in a good word for self-sacrifice and fatigue. For every one book or article I read about our debt of love, I encounter ten others on self-preservation. Burn-out seems to be one of our greatest fears. In my own life I find that sometimes my goal is to protect myself from "stress" more than it is to love others. Granted, we all should have some physical disciplines in our lives to care for our bodies, and we must have some wise, biblically structured priorities in our lives. But we can fall off the cliff of self-preservation as easily as we can the cliff of niceness and people-pleasing.

When we live in the fear of the Lord, there is an intensity to our lives. We are zealous to obey, we are no longer indifferent to others, and we have a desire for the church to be brilliant and outstanding. Such desires may mean some late nights and some tasks we would rather not do. Love is certainly not the easy way out.

Uniqueness in Unity

There is a peculiar change that takes place when you begin to think less about yourself and pursue oneness in the body of Christ. Instead of the members of the church becoming the same, they become more unique. Oneness is not sameness.

If you had asked me to describe Andy, I would have said "boring." He was a friend, and he was part of my local church, but there was nothing really noteworthy about him.

When he asked me for counsel, I can't say that I really looked forward to it. I had even considered saying no, but a few years before I had made a commitment to be more available to people in my local church, so I reluctantly agreed.

His problem was a common one: "I just don't feel good about myself. I want to like myself more." *Oh no,* I thought. *Even the problem he wants to work on is boring.*

When we met for the first time, Andy was expecting the normal counseling questions about his parents and his pain. And maybe I should have asked all those questions, but my heart wasn't in it. Instead, I suggested that we study a book of the Bible together.

I don't even remember what we studied, but I remember it was fun. We both enjoyed it. I remember praying for different people in the church as well as praying together that we would apply the Scripture we were learning. This meant that we prayed a lot, because each week I would learn something from Andy and he from me. One week in particular I remember that he was convicted by his lack of love for his siblings, and he asked for prayer because he was going to ask their forgiveness. I actually started looking forward to our times.

Then one day it hit me. *This guy is colorful,* I thought. *He isn't boring!* Granted, some of the changes could have been in me, but I know it was more than that. Andy and his questions had changed. He had originally asked, "How can I feel better about myself?" Now he was asking, "How can I love people in the church and the world?" The more he applied the biblical teaching on love and oneness, the more apparent his uniqueness became. All of a sudden, I saw gifts in him I had never seen before.

As we were winding down our formal weekly times, I said something that shocked even me. "Andy," I said, "you look beautiful." As the words came out of my mouth I am sure that I was more surprised than Andy. The comment took a little explanation.

"I hope this doesn't sound mean, but as I look back on our relationship, there was a time when I would have said that you were boring—in the best sense of the word, of course." Andy laughed.

"But something has happened to you. I have seen Christ in you over the last four months in a way I have never seen before. I have seen it in your prayers for me and in the strategies you have to love other people. You used to ask, 'How can I feel better about myself?' Now your question is, 'How can I love Christ and love my neighbor?'"

He nodded. He had seen God's work in his life too.

For Further Thought

This chapter reviews an essential part of the treatment for the fear of man: we are to love people more and need people (to satisfy our psychological cravings) less. In the same way that love for God expels the terror of God, love for people expels our fear that they might shame, physically hurt, or reject us.

Family, community, and unity are the key words. But be careful. Christians are not the only ones using them. Have you noticed that many people are getting tired of individualism and self-focus?

Self-interest, self-worth, self-esteem, what's in it for me, the "me" generation, unbridled introspection and personal analysis—we are finally ready for a change. Individualism is out. From a strictly pragmatic perspective, we have found that individualism doesn't work. As an antidote, the new buzz word is *community*.

The problem is that unless there is a radical change in the way we see God, ourselves, and *others*, community will become just another strategy for us to feel better about ourselves. It will relieve the loneliness, and we will feel more "connected," but if we pursue community for self-fulfillment rather than God's glory, the community movement will simply be a passing fad. Let's stir each other up to establish our church community in God's love.

1. How can your church encourage community? How can you encourage community?

2. Review Daniel's "we" prayer, and study Nehemiah's corporate prayer (Neh. 1:4–11). Allow them to structure a corporate prayer time.

3. How can you honor other people in the body of Christ (Rom. 12:10)?

4. Recall the people who have pointed you to Christ recently. Write a letter to one of them, and make a point to tell the others.

CHAPTER

"THE CONCLUSION OF THE MATTER: FEAR GOD AND KEEP HIS COMMANDMENTS"

AN eighteenth-century pastor was bemoaning an epidemic of the fear of man in his church. Everyone, he said, worried more about the opinions of others than they did about God's. Before people in his congregation would do anything, their first question was, "What will *they* think?" The pastor decided to preach a series of sermons on the problem, and he gave this answer: "Fear God and know your duty."

His response was actually two, related answers. The fear of God is the essential foundation. Without this, the fear of man will flourish. The preacher, however, noticed that there were some God-fearing people in the church who were tripped up by the fear of man because they didn't know their duty. That is, they could not discern what form their obedience to God should take. They didn't know how to *apply* the fear of the Lord. As a result, the pastor wisely devoted himself to sermons on various commandments, especially the command to love one another.

The pastor arrived at a very biblical formula:

> Now all has been heard;
>   here is the conclusion of the matter:
> Fear God and keep his commandments,
>   for this is the whole duty of man. (Eccl. 12:13)

I trust that this Puritan pastor soon had people in his church like some of the people I have known.

A *Teenager*

Tim was a popular high school football player—co-captain of the team—who was playing the last few games of his senior year. He was also growing in the fear of the Lord.

What should he do when the football coach announced a special weekend practice that interfered with a planned trip with his family? He didn't know exactly, but he knew the right questions: "What does God want me to do? What is my duty?" After the coach's announcement, he went to the coach and informed him of the conflict.

For the coach, the decision was clear. "What's the problem? The team needs you, and you will be at practice. Only a baby would go with Mommy and Daddy! And if you aren't there, you will be benched for the next game."

For a high school senior, this can certainly arouse the fear of man, but Tim stood firm. He talked with his parents about it, and together they sought the counsel of one of the elders in the church. After hearing some of the biblical perspectives, the teenager decided that he would go with his family on their scheduled trip.

He was keenly aware of the reactions he would get from the coach, and, sure enough, he got them. The coach couldn't believe it. He ranted and raved, trying to get Tim to change his mind, but he didn't. He tried to turn the team against Tim, hoping that peer pressure would reverse his decision, but Tim graciously explained his decision to a team who, for the most part, understood.

He was persuaded of the best biblical course. What more was there to think about? For this teen, there was no decision: "Should I fear God or men?" The answer was obvious: "Fear God and discern my duty."

It would make an interesting story if I could add that the coach repented of his decision to bench Tim, teammates were converted, Tim went on to get a football scholarship, and a movie is being made about his life. But as far as I know, those things didn't happen. He was benched, and that was about it. But to me, it is a glamorous, courageous story that caught the attention of spiritual beings and powers. Tim was placed at the crossroads, faced with the decision of who he was going to fear, and he never hesitated. The impact on spiritual powers, friends, and his church will be much greater than having a few extra tackles marked down on his football record.

A Monk: Martin Luther

Martin Luther had moments of hesitation, but he consistently chose to fear God rather than man. Born in Germany in 1483, Martin Luther was a colorful and influential reformer of the church. But for all his accomplishments, it is his fear of the Lord that stands out in bold relief. His growth in this fear is illustrated by three different incidents.

The first was on July 2, 1505, when Luther was a twenty-one-year-old student at the University of Erfurt. Until that time, Luther had planned to complete his degree and then, following his father's wishes, study law. But as he was returning home to visit his parents, he was caught in a fierce thunderstorm. The lightning was so close that Luther feared for his life and cried out, "St. Anne, help me! I will become a monk."

Even though his vow was spoken without apparent forethought, Luther took it seriously. He believed that his vow was part of a call from heaven that he could not disobey. Therefore, against the wishes of his father (whom Luther had always hoped to please), on July 17 Luther entered the Black Cloister of the Augustinian Hermits in Erfurt.

His fear of the Lord was not mature at this point. It was almost exclusively a fear of the All-Terrible God, and it was mixed with myth-generated fears of fiendish little creatures who supposedly inhabited the woods. But it demonstrated that Martin Luther had a sense of the Holy, and he was more afraid of the Holy than he was of his father's displeasure or his own future discomfort in a monastery.

A second crisis occurred in 1507 after he was selected to the priesthood. The occasion was the first Mass at which he would be the officiating priest. The date was set but then postponed so that Luther's father could attend. This gave the moment an even weightier significance to Luther.

The Mass was (and is) considered to be a re-enactment of Calvary where the priest transforms the bread and wine into the actual flesh and blood of Christ. In other words, the priest was as close as possible to the presence of the Holy. There were extensive guidelines for the priests, used as safety precautions, and the Mass had been celebrated thousands of times before, but these assurances did not comfort Luther. God was still the All-Terrible. He was attractive in some ways, but he was more to be avoided than embraced. Therefore, Luther was nearly dumbstruck when he began the ceremony.

I was utterly stupefied and terror-stricken. I thought to myself, "With what tongue shall I address such Majesty, seeing that all men ought to tremble in the presence of even an earthly prince? Who am I, that I should lift up mine eyes to raise my hands to the divine majesty? The angels surround him. At his nod the earth trembles. And shall I, a miserable pygmy, say, 'I want this, I ask for that'? For I am dust and ashes and full of sin and I am speaking to the living, eternal and true God."[1]

Luther, somehow, was able to finish.

There is some progress here. Luther is following the great tradition of Isaiah and others who were awed by the presence of God. King David, who certainly knew of God's love, was so awed by God that he indicated that it even took courage to pray (2 Sam. 7:27). But for Luther, there was still no clear link between God's justice and his love.

To bridge the gap between justice and love, Luther tried working harder. Like most people, he thought that he could earn God's love. Therefore, he pursued personal holiness with a diligence second to none. He tried it all: three-day fasts, six-hour confessions, nights sleeping in the cold without blankets, and constant prayer, all to the point where he should have been dead. But tranquillity was not forthcoming.

Yet God was clearly at work in the monk's life. Luther was a fine scholar who studied the biblical languages and the Scriptures themselves. In 1509 he received the degree of bachelor of biblical studies, and in 1512 he received the degree of doctor of theology. These studies prepared him for his appointment as professor of Bible at Wittenberg, where his responsibility was to give exegetical

---

1 Roland Bainton, *Here I Stand: A Life of Martin Luther* (New York: New American Library, 1950), 30.

lectures on the biblical books. With this task, he was, as they say, a pig in mud.

In 1513–15 he lectured on the Psalms, in 1515–16 on Romans, in 1516–17 on Galatians, and in 1517–18 on Hebrews. The gospel was becoming clearer. He saw Christ as the All-Merciful One in the Psalms. Then, when he studied Romans, everything clicked. "Justification by faith alone," became Luther's summary of the work of God in salvation. In Christ, Luther was finally knowing God as All-Just *and* All-Merciful.

> I greatly longed to understand Paul's Epistle to the Romans and nothing stood in my way but that one expression, "the justice of God," because I took it to mean that justice whereby God is just and deals justly in punishing the unjust. My situation was that, although an impeccable monk, I stood before God as a sinner troubled in conscience, and I had no confidence that my merit would assuage him. Therefore I did not love a just and angry God, but rather hated and murmured against him. Yet I clung to dear Paul and had a great yearning to know what he meant.
>
> Night and day I pondered until I saw the connection between the justice of God and the statement that "the just shall live by his faith." Then I grasped that the justice of God is that righteousness by which through grace and sheer mercy God justifies us through faith. Thereupon I felt myself to be reborn and to have gone through open doors into paradise. . . . This is to behold God in faith, that you should look upon his fatherly, friendly heart, in which there is no anger nor ungraciousness. He who sees God as angry does not see him rightly but looks only on a curtain, as if a dark cloud had been drawn across his face.[2]

2 Ibid., 50.

A robust fear of the Lord had been nurtured by study and meditation in the Scriptures. It would soon be tested.

Luther is best known for his reaction against indulgences. In his day, the church would often raise money by selling what were perceived to be divine favors. If you gave money when the indulgences were being offered, you could release relatives and yourself from purgatory. This system so violated the principle of justification by faith that Luther felt compelled to respond. He did so by posting the Ninety-five Theses on the door of the Castle Church in Wittenberg.

These theses, along with dozens of subsequent publications, put Luther at such odds with the Roman Catholic Church that he was in constant danger. Either his enemies would try to assassinate him, or the church would burn him as a heretic. Whatever the means, Luther assumed that death was inevitable. His books were already being publicly burned in Rome. Yet these threats did not keep Luther from writing more pamphlets supporting what he understood to be the words of God himself.

Church trials did not give Luther the opportunity to debate. Instead, they were attacks on Luther, demanding that he recant his writings and humbly submit to the church. Luther even "recanted" at one point.

> I was wrong, I admit it, when I said that indulgences were "the pious defrauding of the faithful." I recant and say, "Indulgences are the most impious frauds and impostors of the most rascally pontiffs, by which they deceive the souls and destroy the goods of the faithful."

Such sarcasm multiplied both his friends and enemies.

Luther's final appeal eventually led to a meeting before a prestigious assembly at Worms. After many reversals of decisions as to whether Luther should be allowed to speak or not, on April 16, 1521,

Luther arrived in Worms. The hoped-for debate was simply a public trial. Luther would not be given opportunity to lecture on his conclusions. After displaying Luther's books, the examiner asked a simple question: "Do you defend them all, or do you care to reject a part?"

Luther's response was curious, especially in light of his bold writings. Perhaps he was intimidated by the collection of the most powerful men ever assembled in that area. "To say too little or too much would be dangerous," he replied in a barely audible voice. "I beg you, give me time to think it over."

He seemed to be teetering between the fear of man and the fear of the Lord, but something happened by six o'clock the next evening. Luther demonstrated the boldness that was characteristic of his writings. Such boldness was not self-confidence, because he was a man who walked humbly before God, but it was a confidence in God's Word.

In his remarks, he defended his writings and told the men who had the power to kill him, "I must walk in the fear of the Lord." He ended his comments by stating, "My conscience is captive to the Word of God. I cannot and I will not recant anything, for to go against conscience is neither right nor safe. God help me. Here I stand, I cannot do otherwise. Amen."

Luther demonstrated that it is possible to fear the Lord at the same time that you are afraid. After all, he was appearing before an august tribunal with great spiritual and political power. No wonder he was afraid! But, in the midst of his fear, he chose to trust and obey God. That is the fear of the Lord in a most elegant form.

A Hebrew Prophet and His Friends

Luther's role models had to be the men of the book of Daniel: Daniel, Shadrach, Meshach, and Abednego. Other than Jesus himself, there are no greater models of the fear of the Lord. These men rose to prominence during the worst of times for the remnants of Israel. The northern kingdom was gone, and Babylon had invaded Judah and established puppet kings. At the beginning of Babylon's occupation, they took the best and brightest from Judah's royal family to serve in Nebuchadnezzar's court, among them Daniel and his friends.

How Daniel learned the fear of the Lord is not certain. The Judean king who reigned during the Babylonian occupation was the wicked king Jehoiakim, and he was preceded by the brief reign of another wicked king. However, fourteen years before the Babylonian captivity, Josiah had been king, and he had brought revival to the kingdom. It is likely that Daniel and his three friends were raised in the spirit of Josiah.

The danger with the book of Daniel is that our familiarity with the stories and the apparent ease with which these men chose the fear of the Lord make the book sound very ordinary. For example, the book begins with Daniel's refusal to eat the king's assigned food. To eat such food would have brought defilement according to the Mosaic law, and Daniel chose to follow that law. For Daniel, his duty was obvious.

But Daniel could easily have been sentenced to death for his refusal to eat the king's food. He was a captive Hebrew, and Nebuchadnezzar certainly would not have tolerated such a troublemaker. Given the circumstances I suspect that many people would have fudged on the law, rationalizing that some laws were more important than others. I'm sure that the Pharisees could have managed a conscience-appeasing re-interpretation of the law within minutes. Why make an issue out of unclean food or food and wine that had been sacrificed to an idol? But it was absolutely clear to Daniel. "He asked the chief official for permission not to defile himself this way" (Dan.

1:8). Yet this was just a courtesy. No matter what the chief official would say, Daniel had determined his course of action.

The fear of the Lord simplifies life.

It is as if the book of Daniel is the fear of the Lord's Hall of Fame. Next were the three Hebrews—Shadrach, Meshach, and Abednego. They were told to worship a large statue of Nebuchadnezzar. The directions were very clear: When you hear music, fall down and worship the image. If you don't, you will immediately be thrown into a blazing furnace.

The biblical text doesn't mention how Nebuchadnezzar's cronies actually saw the Hebrews disregard the decree, but since the three Hebrews were men of some prominence, their disregard of the edict must have been obvious. They were immediately brought before a furious king. As a gesture of unprecedented mercy, Nebuchadnezzar gave the men an opportunity to recant and do it his way, but the men did not even need the night to think about it.

Their reply to the king's offer is absolutely astonishing.

> *O Nebuchadnezzar, we do not need to defend ourselves before you in this matter. If we are thrown into the blazing furnace, the God we serve is able to save us from it, and he will rescue us from your hand, O king. But even if he does not, we want you to know, O king, that we will not serve your gods or worship the image of gold you have set up. (Dan. 3:16–18)*

The fact that they lived through the furnace is, to me, anticlimactic. That God could raise up men like this is enough. They are evidence of his great power.

The third prominent story about the fear of man involved Daniel again. Whereas pride was the reason for Nebuchadnezzar's edict that condemned the three Hebrew men, jealousy was the motive behind the royal decree that affected Daniel. Daniel was one of those remarkable men who had great God-given talent, an impeccable reputation, and an unceasing fear of the Lord. It is a rare combination that would provoke envy in many people, so it was not surprising that Daniel's administrative and ruling peers were beside themselves with jealousy.

But how could they ever "get" Daniel? Everyone has his Achilles' heel. If you spy long enough on anyone, you should be able to find something that would mar his reputation and keep him out of power. But these men knew that "unless it has something to do with the law of God," they would never be able to trap him.

Perhaps taking a page out of the annals of Nebuchadnezzar's reign, the rulers suggested that King Darius issue an irrevocable edict, enforced for only one month, that would prohibit prayer to any man or god other than the king. Darius was satisfied with the suggestion but completely unaware of its implications.

As before, Daniel made it look easy. He didn't take a day to think about it. Instead, he just continued his thrice-daily habit of praying on his knees by an open window that faced Jerusalem. He was not trying to make a spectacle of himself with such public praying. Rather, he faced Jerusalem because of his great love for his people and the promises of God to Jerusalem. He would offer prayers of thanks and, undoubtedly, prayers that the Messiah who would forgive and deliver his people would soon come.

There is no record of what Daniel said prior to being sealed within the den of lions. It's too bad. His comments would have made for great drama. But Daniel, who authored the book, was certainly not one to draw attention to himself. I am sure that he had to go through agony as he considered what was about to happen. Like his Hebrew friends, he knew God *could* deliver him, but he also knew that such deliverance was unlikely.

Daniel was not interested in drawing attention to himself. Instead, he wanted us to know that God was greater than kings, greater than fire, and greater even than underfed lions. He wanted God's name to be hallowed in all the world, and it was. After God spared Daniel, Darius punished the jealous administrators along with their families, and he issued another edict:

> In every part of my kingdom people must fear and reverence the God of Daniel.

> For he is the living God
>   and he endures forever;
> his kingdom will not be destroyed,
>   his dominion will never end.
> He rescues and he saves;
>   he performs signs and wonders
>   in the heavens and on the earth.
> He has rescued Daniel
>   from the power of the lions. (Dan. 6:26–27)

A Housewife: Nancy

Nancy is not a biblical character. She is a twenty-seven-year-old wife and mother of two who said she was absolutely desperate.

Having grown up with a drunken father and a mother who ignored her pleas for help when her father was cruel, Nancy felt worthless and empty. She came to her pastor because she felt that her husband wasn't meeting her needs, and, as a result, she alternated between anger and depression.

Without question, it is tragic to have a history of cruelty and neglect in your family, and Nancy needed to understand what God says to people who have been hurt by others. Yet this is only part of the necessary biblical foundation. If Nancy's sense of worthlessness and emptiness revealed a view of herself as a leaky love cup, then she also needed to be reforged into a different kind of vessel.

One reason Christians respond positively to a need psychology is that it takes people's pain seriously. However, this perspective can actually make pain worse. It compounds pain by suggesting that not only did the sins of others hurt deeply, but they also deprived you of something—a right, something you were owed—that is necessary for life. Being deeply hurt by others is hard enough, but when we believe that their sin was a near-lethal blow that damaged the core of our being, the hurt is intensified. For example, if someone robs us of valuable jewelry it is very troubling, but if these jewels were our only financial resource for our upcoming retirement, then the felt loss is much greater. Therefore, one task in counseling is to begin to separate the real hurt from the pain that is amplified by our own lusts and longings. The result will be simple, godly grief.

The pastor began by teaching Nancy about God's compassion on those who have been sinned against by others. His goal was to surprise Nancy with God's holy love for her. While sharing God's perspective on victims with Nancy, the pastor also asked her to consider three questions. The first was, "What do you need?" After a short time of reflection, Nancy answered, "I need my husband to listen to me and meet my emotional needs."

The pastor responded with an observation that has been made throughout history. "Nancy, have you ever noticed that we tend to be controlled by the things we need? Can you see this working in your relationship with your husband? As long as you need your husband to fill you emotionally, you will feel controlled by him."

The second question built on that observation. The pastor asked Nancy to consider the question, "What or who controls you?" She was asked to be especially alert to events or people that left her depressed or angry.

She came back with quite a list. It included her husband, children, mother, father, and friends at church. She had written down events from each day that demonstrated to her that she was controlled by other people.

Then she was given a third question: "Where do you put your trust?"

Nancy immediately saw that the three questions were identical. What she needed controlled her; what controlled her was the object of her trust or fear. Her past was certainly troubled and painful, and it needed to be dealt with. But the issue that made her life so difficult now was not her past as much as it was the object of her worship. The problem was within her, not outside her.

Nancy began to pinpoint her problem as a fear of man and a lack of fear of God. Like so many Christians, *people* had become the controlling point of Nancy's life. She held others in awe. She put her hope in them. Furthermore, as in all cases of the fear of man, *self*-concern was the force behind it. She relied on others because she believed they had the power to give her what she wanted. She needed people because of what *she* wanted. In other words, other people were big because her desires were big.

Nancy began to distinguish between shame from being sinned against and shame from her own sin. Of the two, she began to realize that the shame from her own sin was more serious. As deep as her pain was, she realized that her sin problem was deeper than her pain problem.

Certainly, she saw a number of obvious sins in her life, but she was most troubled by the deep theme of the fear of man that came out of her own heart. She was worshipping others for her own purposes. This, she found, was perhaps the dominant sin pattern in her life.

With this at the core, she knew that the answer was not to turn to Christ to meet her felt need. That would have made Jesus her personal talisman or idol. Instead, her answer was to put to death her selfish desires and to learn to fear God alone. As a result, her question began to change. It was no longer "Where can I find my worth?" but "Why am I so concerned about myself?" It was not "How can God fill my needs?" but "How can I see Christ as so glorious that I forget about my perceived needs?"

She found Jeremiah 17:5–10 especially helpful. It showed that the fear of man was the real cause of her emptiness. It was a curse that left its victims destitute or empty. The alternative, trust in God, was a blessing that led to life and *fullness.*

She began to pray the Lord's Prayer. When praying, "Forgive me my debts," she often thought of times when her husband had taken the place of God. She confessed that she had been approaching marriage as a way to meet felt needs. She confessed that her husband had been her designated need-meeter. Such times of confession would have been like self-inflicted wounds in the past, but now, with a greater understanding of God's holy love, they were liberating.

She also began to pray for the fear of the Lord. She knew that confession would not, in itself, make God bigger than people in her life. With confidence that God would grant her more of the fear of the Lord, she began searching Scripture for awesome pictures of God. She went to Isaiah 6, Ezekiel 1, and the book of Revelation. She began looking for glory around her during her day. She even read C. S. Lewis's *The Chronicles of Narnia* as a way to think more about her mighty God.

As she developed a more brilliant "scrapbook" of pictures of God, Nancy was gradually coming to understand *her* true shape. The leaky love cup was on its way out, even though it would emerge many more times. It was being replaced by God-given images such as friend, wise one, prophet, priest, king, and spouse. She even identified pictures such as servant or slave to Christ. But she especially saw herself as a Christian.

Nancy was learning the fear of the Lord, and she was understanding the nature of her own heart. There was only one part remaining: what was her duty toward others? Her pastor never specifically discussed this because Nancy had already raced ahead toward loving others. No longer did she talk as if other people owed her. Instead, she began to think about creative ways to love. Her question became fairly simple, "What is my duty before the God who has loved me?"

For Nancy, her duty meant a number of things. Under the heading of love, she looked for the log in her own eye before she spoke to her husband about his specks. Then she told him about the way some of his actions had hurt her. Her gentleness and obvious concern for their relationship made her words easy for him to hear. Together, they began to pray about how to love her parents, and they sought the counsel of other friends at church.

She decided that she would approach her non-Christian parents this way:

> ➤ She would share what she had been learning about herself and the fear of the Lord (as far as her parents were interested in hearing).

> ➤ She would ask their forgiveness for specific ways she had sinned against them, and she would invite them to raise issues that she neglected.

> ➤ She would talk to her parents privately about how they too had sinned, and add that she had forgiven them. She also

decided to ask her parents if they wanted to speak more specifically about past events. If so, she would be happy to speak with them.

The pastor then blessed her with God's Word: "God has poured out his love into our hearts by the Holy Spirit, whom he has given us" (Rom. 5:5). This may sound strange after all we've said about rejecting a need-based, love cup view of the person. Is Scripture saying that we are love cups after all? Not really. Although the metaphor of a cup is in plain view, it is a cup that is spiritually, not psychologically, needy. The context clarifies the exact nature of this love: "While we were still sinners, Christ died for us" (Rom. 5:8). When we recognize that people come to God in the shape of desperately needy sinners in need of grace, all counselors should seek to deluge the counselee with the love of Christ. If you are the counselor, this should be your greatest joy: to pour and pour God's love over those who are spiritually parched. This, after all, will bring great glory to the name of Christ.

A Counselor-Teacher

Having been instructed by God's Word and surrounded by such impressive examples as Tim, Martin Luther, and Nancy, I too am gradually learning to fear God rather than man.

When my wife rightly rebukes me, I am able to listen and learn—usually. When I feel like an abject failure, rather than mope around for a few days I am quicker to ask, "What is my duty?"

Let me give you a before and after picture that I hope will encourage you.

I was teaching a class at the Christian Counseling and Educational Foundation where I work. The course had its ups and downs, but one particular lecture was especially down. Even I found it boring.

Have you ever been at an elementary school when the end-of-school bell rings? It looks something like the running of the bulls in Spain. It looks like children have literally exploded out of the building, released from prison. Of course, such behavior wanes as children get older.

When the bell rang ending my class—waking a few of my eager pupils—the students looked as if they were back in elementary school. I had never seen a classroom empty so quickly. It probably created a backdraft—the kind you feel when a truck goes by. No one asked a question. No one said good-bye.

I drove home, sat at the dining room table, and immediately started looking in the want ads, hoping to find a job where I didn't have to see or talk to a person.

"Woe is me," I thought. "What a horrible failure. I am humiliated. I don't ever want to see those students again."

As I browsed through the paper, looking like a little boy who lost his dog (and hoping that my wife would ask me what was wrong), my wife finally did ask why I looked so blue. After hearing the pitiful tale, she gave some great counsel.

"Stop that," she said. "You have responsibilities to your students."

It wasn't exactly the counsel that I wanted to hear. I wanted to be filled with sympathy and unconditional love. "Oh Honey, I'm sure class was great, and even if it wasn't, I still think you are great. . . ." If she would have asked, I could have scripted her response. But she chose something that went more directly to the heart.

"Stop that" was exactly what I needed. It was shorthand for, "Why are you so consumed with yourself? I want you to be liberated from self-concern by fearing God and knowing your duty."

Sheri's wake-up call sent me on a new course. I began to look more seriously at the selfishness and pride that lurked right below my woe-is-me exterior. It wasn't pretty. As John Calvin suggested, I wasn't a love cup; I was an idol factory. I wanted to worship something or someone that would give me glory. Not too much glory, of course. Just enough to make me feel good about myself. If my student-idols could have just asked a few good questions after class and not left in such a rush, that would have been enough—for then.

My cup was filled with *me*. It was not empty.

Hand-in-hand with these insights into my deceitful heart was a deeper understanding of God's forgiveness. In fact, it may have been the first time that I realized that God's forgiveness of me was a holy forgiveness, so holy that he was to be feared. I was amazed and blessed by the love of God for me as a sinner. Armed with such confidence in his forgiving love, I could pray even more boldly that God would continue to search me and expose my heart.

The next six months were not filled with painful introspection. Instead, they were good times of biblically guided self-examination helped by the counsel of family and friends. There were no bursts of insight, just gradual clarity on issues of the heart.

I found that pride ran deep. Beneath the despondency of little failures was the desire to be somebody. I wanted to be the great teacher. I wanted to be filled with the respect of my students. I wanted to have the most popular classes. "*I want. . . .*"

I found that people were big, my desires for self-glory were even bigger, and God was small. I cared more about the praise of men than the praise of God. I was a worshipper of people, hoping that they would give me the blessing I desired. I found that I needed my class *for my purposes* more than I loved them. The path away from the fear of man was the path of confession of sin and repentance. There were no other options.

The test came about three years later. It was the middle of the semester and I was teaching a class. It was going okay, but one lecture was just a bomb. I felt as if I was giving information that had no point. If I could have fallen asleep, I would have. Instead, I just let a polite but drowsy class leave a few minutes early.

The ride home was . . . different. I wasn't thinking, "What are those students thinking about me?" Instead, I began to consider my duty. I realized that I needed to spend more time in preparation for the next class. I wanted to get home so that I could get to work on the lecture for next week. I realized that God had called me to teach that semester, and I was certain he had more in mind than simply humbling me. I believed that he wanted me to teach and disciple my students. I was committed to going into the next class prepared, excited about what I was teaching, and changed by it personally.

It was a great week. It was a week of liberation from the snares of the fear of man. Instead of being consumed with self-doubt and self-pity, I asked my wife and other friends to pray for the lecture. Of course, I prayed too. I probably prayed more that week than I had in months. But it wasn't the "make it a success" prayer that I have often prayed. It was "May your name be glorified and may students grow in the knowledge of yourself and obedience to you."

Certainly, I have stumbled since then, but there is no going back to the reclusive days of high school. I now have the awesome (fearful) presence of God. I live under his gaze. Do you remember the gaze? The gaze that exposes nakedness and uncleanness? This is a different gaze.

It is the gaze of acceptance. It was experienced by the Israelites who had blood on their doors. When the blood was seen, the angel of death passed by.

It is the gaze that sees covering from guilt and shame. The Father, who always keeps his word, says that he forgives and cleanses. When he says that he will glorify his name through us, he will do it.

It is the gaze of protection and power. It came from the King who loves to give us the kingdom (Luke 12:32).

It is the gaze of the bridegroom who loves to give the best of gifts to his bride, and the very best gift is his presence, the Holy Spirit (Luke 11:13).

This is the gaze that transforms. It will expel the fear of man and be a blessing for all God's people. As God's priests, we should pray for it for our spouse, friends, children, and the entire church.

> *The LORD bless you*
> *and keep you;*
> *the LORD make his face shine upon you*
> *and be gracious to you;*
> *the LORD turn his face toward you*
> *and give you peace. (Num. 6:24–26)*

Edward T. Welch serves both the Christian Counseling and Educational Foundation (CCEF) and Westminster Theological Seminary. At CCEF he is, in addition to being a counselor and faculty member, the director of counseling and academic dean. At Westminster he is professor of practical theology. He joined both organizations in 1981.

In addition to writing *Addictions* and *Blame It on the Brain*, Welch has contributed to several books, including *What's the Brain Got to Do with It?*, *Our Smallest Members*, *Leadership Handbook of Practical Theology* (vol. 2), and *Power Religion*.

Welch has written more than ten articles for the *Journal of Biblical Counseling*. Other periodicals to carry his essays include *Journal of Psychology and Christianity*, *Journal of Pastoral Practice*, *Journal of Biblical Ethics in Medicine*, *Carer and Counselor*, *Modern Reformation*, *New Horizons*, *American Family Association Journal*, *Spiritual Counterfeits Project Journal*, *Reforma Siglo*, and *Westminster Bulletin*.

At meetings of such organizations as the Christian Association for Psychological Studies, American Association of Christian Counselors, and Pennsylvania Psychological Association, Welch has presented papers.

After earning his M.Div. degree at Biblical Theological Seminary, Welch received, in 1981, a Ph.D. in counseling psychology (neuropsychology) from the University of Utah.

RESOURCES FOR CHANGING LIVES

Addictions—A Banquet in the Grave: Finding Hope in the Power of the Gospel. Edward T. Welch shows how addictions result from a worship disorder—idolatry—and how they are overcome by the power of the gospel. *978-0-87552-606-5*

Age of Opportunity: A Biblical Guide to Parenting Teens, 2d ed. Paul David Tripp uncovers the heart issues affecting parents' relationship with their teenagers. *978-0-87552-605-8*

Blame It on the Brain? Distinguishing Chemical Imbalances, Brain Disorders, and Disobedience. Edward T. Welch compares the roles of the brain and the heart in problems such as alcoholism, depression, ADD, and homosexuality. *978-0-87552-602-7*

Instruments in the Redeemer's Hands: People in Need of Change Helping People in Need of Change. Paul David Tripp demonstrates how God uses his people, who need change themselves, as tools of change in the lives of others. *978-0–87552–607–2*

Seeing with New Eyes: Counseling and the Human Condition through the Lens of Scripture. David Powlison embraces, probes, and unravels counseling and the problems of daily life with a biblical perspective. *978-0-87552-608-9*

Step by Step: Divine Guidance for Ordinary Christians. James C. Petty sifts through approaches to knowing God's will and illustrates how to make biblically wise decisions. *978-0-87552-603-4*

War of Words: Getting to the Heart of Your Communication Struggles. Paul David Tripp takes us beyond superficial solutions in the struggle to control our tongues. *978-0-87552-604-1*

When People Are Big and God Is Small: Overcoming Peer Pressure, Codependency, and the Fear of Man. Edward T. Welch exposes the spiritual dimensions of pride, defensiveness, people-pleasing, needing approval, "self-esteem," etc. *978-0-87552-600-3*

Booklet Series: *A.D.D.; Anger; Angry at God?; Bad Memories; Depression; Domestic Abuse; Forgiveness; God's Love; Guidance; Homosexuality; "Just One More"; Marriage; Motives; OCD; Pornography; Pre-Engagement; Priorities; Procrastination; Self-Injury; Sexual Sin; Stress; Suffering; Suicide; Teens and Sex; Thankfulness; Why Me?; Worry*

FOR FURTHER INFORMATION

Speaking engagements with authors in this series may be arranged by calling The Christian Counseling and Educational Foundation at (215) 884-7676.

Videotapes and audio cassettes by authors in this series may be ordered through Resources for Changing Lives at (800) 318-2186.

For a complete catalog of titles from P&R Publishing, call (800) 631-0094.